THE SAMURAI LISTENER

Amy,
Welcome to PPS.
So Glad you
Joined us!
Pease Let me
Know if
I can Help

BY CASH NICKERSON

Post Hill PRESS

A POST HILL PRESS BOOK
ISBN: 978-1-68261-525-6
ISBN (eBook): 978-1-68261-526-3

Cover art by Tricia Principe, principedesign.com

Post Hill Press
New York · Nashville
posthillpress.com

Published in the United States of America

DEDICATION

THIS BOOK IS dedicated to those who are continuously dissatisfied with their performance and seek to improve their skills, gifts, and talents.

It is dedicated to those who approach each day determined to make it a better day than the last.

It is dedicated to those who lead others and spend their time trying to improve those around them.

Imagine a world where we each help the other, and in constructive ways we work to improve our ability to work together to advance humanity.

I am humbly engaged in the effort to help dramatically improve how we work with one another on a day-to-day basis with a view towards making work more fun, productive, and successful.

Cash

ACKNOWLEDGEMENTS

I WANT TO acknowledge all of my martial arts instructors and training partners, especially Vladmir Vasiliev, all of the Machado family, Martin Wheeler, and Rick Fowler. I also want to acknowledge my academic professors at Carleton College in Northfield, Minnesota, and my law school and graduate business school professors at Washington University in St. Louis.

Special thanks to Debra Englander who helped me by editing drafts of the book and to Billie Brownell and the other editors and staff at Post Hill Press. We all need those who make us do one more try, one more effort, and one more draft.

TABLE OF CONTENTS

LEARNING THE "HIDDEN ARTS"

THOSE OF US who have been in the workplace for a long time know that soft skills matter. I use the term "soft skills" (compared to "hard skills") to mean the interpersonal and social skills of a person working in an organization, not their skills in their trade or craft. We all have witnessed the rise of certain people in organizations who we know are not necessarily the most technically competent. To be sure, they are technically proficient, but they are not the best coders, lawyers, accountants, operators, or engineers in the companies they eventually lead. They could be, but they usually aren't.

Generally, we have come to accept this fact without questioning or examining it. We take it as a given in the human behavior in organizations ecosystem that "people skills" or "soft skills" is a defining factor in success. That begs the question: If there is something besides your technical skills that is a key factor in how far you rise in an organization, what is it? Why do some people have it while others don't? We don't consider it unfair; mostly, we acknowledge that accomplishing undertakings and leading others to do so takes a different set of skills than the technical skills we learn in colleges and universities and on our on-the-job skills training. But where do you acquire these other skills? Are they innate? Where do you turn for instruction in the art of getting things done and leading others to do so?

That's a great question, but unfortunately there are not a lot of easy answers. We tend to treat soft skills as "hidden arts," somewhat like martial arts. We often view soft skills as something with which you are born or otherwise mysteriously acquire. We consider them talents.

Have you noticed that some people can walk into a room and immediately "take over the room"? Everyone in the room becomes attentive and wants to hear what that person has to say. Those same people seem to be able to say, "Let's go *this* way," and everyone follows them. Those same people speak and those around them say, "I could listen to them all day long."

It's natural to want to be one of those people who attracts others and whom people admire. And here is the good news: Not everyone is born with this talent. You can study and learn these traits. I learned the hard way, largely because of my first job review decades ago that I didn't like or understand.

My first job review in the professional workplace was in 1985, when I was a young corporate lawyer at the Union Pacific Railroad. It was a mediocre review, which I am convinced had nothing whatsoever to do with my legal skills. How were my legal technical skills? They were first rate; I ranked highly in my class and I was an Articles Editor of the Law Review. I clerked for one of the top professors at my school. I interned for one of the top law firms in the country and the largest in the region where I went to law school. I was hired by the Union Pacific Railroad, one of the oldest, most prestigious and conservative companies in the United States, after a national search for one of two new lawyers. (Abraham Lincoln signed the Pacific Railroad Act of 1862 on July 1, 1862, which created the Union Pacific Railroad.)

But according to my first-year review, among my other flaws, I had "soft skills" issues. At the time of that review, nobody referred to them as soft skills. But the criticisms in the written review and in a conversation about the review were clearly about what I now understand were soft skill issues: I was aloof and too task oriented. I was not a people person. I had excelled at every project, but I hadn't paid attention to the environment in which I worked at the time. Out of habit I suppose, I treated the workplace like it was school. Law school back then was very much like the way it was characterized in the movie *The Paper Chase*. It was competitive. While there were study groups, it still was a "me against everyone else" type of environment.

The review bewildered me. My first boss, Bill Higgins, who was responsible for the review, was a former WWII Army infantryman who had fought at The Battle of the Bulge; he liked my work and me. But as I sought to glean clues from my environment, I could tell his assistant *didn't* like me. She looked at me with disdain whenever I entered or left his office. It took me months to figure out that she was my primary critic and she was influential.

And that is one reason, I discovered, for the mediocre review. She had helped create the reputation I had acquired for being too intense and not very human. Since this assistant was popular, she successfully held me back as she shared her view of me with others in the environment and apparently, everything I did constantly confirmed her opinion. It wouldn't be fair to blame her alone, because she was just more observant. She was right. I didn't care about other people in the workplace enough; I cared too much about my own work and getting it exactly right. I aimed for perfection. I had carried over the intense competitive skills I had developed in school that had worked for me and brought them into the workplace.

This negative review had nothing to do with my work. I later learned that Jim Dolan, my manager's boss, the VP of Law, had to encourage my boss to include more positive comments in my review because of the work I actually did. Nevertheless, at the young age of 26, what held me back were skills I had not learned in college, law school, or business school. My behaviors in the office and the perception of those behaviors by my boss' assistant and everyone else in the office who had an opinion had derailed me—possibly even threatened my career.

I suspected there were underlying and mysterious factors at play in my review because it made no rational sense to me. How could I do great work and get a mediocre review? It wasn't as if I were a bad person. I hadn't done anything to hurt anyone else. There were clearly unwritten rules at work, but I didn't know what they were or where to find them. There were "hidden arts." I knew nothing of the "hidden arts." So I turned my perceived intensity into a desire to understand and master these "hidden arts."

This book is intended to share what I have learned about the "hidden arts" over the past thirty-five years in every imaginable type of professional setting from start-up enterprises, to big corporations, to midsized companies, as well as law firms of all sizes. Perhaps, most important, my primary industry expertise has been in the area of employment. I have been involved with human resources, talent acquisition, recruiting, and merging and acquiring companies that perform such tasks for a very long time.

Simultaneously, in my personal life, I have been a student of many types of martial arts. I have studied and taught martial arts as a hobby and business. I studied Shotokan Karate in my youth and then American Kenpo Karate, achieving a third-degree black belt. I studied kickboxing under a world champion kickboxer. I have studied for more than ten years and continue to study Brazilian Jiu Jitsu with the Machado family, cousins to the Gracie's, obtaining a brown belt thus far. I have studied Systema, the Russian Martial Arts, for more than ten years under Vladmir Vasiliev. Most recently I studied Iaido, the Samurai Martial Art, in Tokyo, Japan, under a real samurai.

My greatest contribution to this study of soft skills as "hidden arts" is my recognition of a clear and instructive parallel between martial arts, which themselves were hidden arts, and the "hidden arts" of the workplace. I am a lifelong student of many martial arts and not so long ago, I recognized the parallels and insights that could be drawn from the study of both. Although these parallels developed over the life of my career, they consciously aligned as I studied the soft skill of listening during 2014. That study culminated in a series of essays that I published in a book called *Listening as A Martial Art*, which focused on growth in techniques related to listening. I barely scratched the surface of the topic, but reactions to those essays convinced me there was a need for a comprehensive book on soft skills, especially communication. My essays in *Listening as a Martial Art* got me thinking more deeply about listening, which led to the ARE U PRESENT listening approach developed in this book.

In this book I look at soft skills, particularly the soft skill of communication, much more deeply and I redefine "listening" altogether into the much broader concept of "sensing." With four more years of daily martial arts reading, study, and training, I have refined the parallels between combat arts and workplace arts. Given my advanced martial arts skills as well as my workplace skills, now having been honed over thirty-two-plus years, I am confident I could sense and correct the reaction of my environment to my behavior back in my first job and correct that initial review. I am also confident that armed with my experiences of failures and successes over the years, I could have dramatically improved my batting average of success versus failures.

Even if you're not familiar with martial arts concepts (and you don't need to be to understand and apply the principles of this book), another way to understand the concept of soft skills is to think back to your early days of school. The classroom required and developed one set of behaviors, namely digesting information and learning subjects like history, math, and literature. These skills used and developed our intelligence, or IQ. The playground and recess was about getting along with others on a social basis; perhaps playground skills can be thought of as emotional intelligence. Gym class involved another set of behaviors and skills that involved and developed our physical strength, agility, and stamina. But to bring soft skills to bear in the workplace, one needs to combine physical, social, and mental skills. Perhaps this early separation of the physical, social, and mental is part of the problem and an evolutionary step backwards for us. We will explore that more fully in chapters to come, but regardless, the winners in the workplace, those who become leaders, balance these skills like a three-legged stool.

If you read this book, regularly perform the exercises, and consider the suggested dialogues and reviews at the end of each chapter, you will become an expert in the "hidden arts." You will become a Samurai Listener—someone who can sense opportunity and distinguish it from danger. You will learn what to worry about and what to ignore. You will learn how to handle conflict, how to speak so people will listen, how to listen so people will seek you out, and how to lead. Your next review will be surprisingly better than your last. You will combine your playground/social skills, your physical education skills, and your classroom/intelligence skills. By combining these skills, you will become whole again. You will lead and succeed and become "one of those people."

CHAPTER 1

REDEFINING LISTENING

WHEN WE THINK of listening, we think of hearing. As children, we are constantly asked, "Are you listening?" We are told to "pay attention." When we look away, we may be reminded to, "Look at me when I am talking to you." As we get older and we want someone to pay attention to us, we may say something like, "hey," before we speak. We may say your name as well, "Hey John," followed by something we consider important. I even have friends who say, "Hey listen," before they talk. When we are done saying something we want someone to "hear" we may say, "Got it?" We all have friends who often ask, "We good?" after a statement they want us to get. Good speakers seek to let you know what they say is important and check at the end to see if you have really "heard" them. This is an important trait of good listeners. But you'll find there is so much more to listening than hearing when you actually take time to think about it.

You are in a meeting. Someone is speaking. The others are "listening." You are "listening." What are you watching? Are you looking at the speaker's lips? Are you watching his gestures? Are you looking at his face? Are you scanning the room for reactions from others? Are you open to what is being said? Are you engaged and nodding or smiling? What is the speaker's body posture or gestures? What is your posture? Do you understand the speaker? Is your mind wandering? Are you staying focused? Is there some resolution or conclusion to the communication? What emotions do you bring to the topic? How many of your other senses are engaged? How does the speaker or other listeners or the topic or content affect you or your ego? Are you nervous about the topic or the presence of the other participants? How is the timing or tempo of the entire communication?

You may be sitting in that meeting thinking you're hearing the speaker but you're doing a lot more than physically "hearing." How you are behaving in that situation, in that meeting, is the result of habits you have formed over the years from sitting in many meetings or conversations you've had, or maybe even from comments managers have made to you. Whatever habits you have, they have remained active because you subconsciously believe they have worked for you. That is, you think these habits have helped you succeed or advance in your career. They are not even conscious. I urge you think to think about these habits. Are they good habits? Or are they bad habits? When is the last time you actively tried to change those habits to improve your "listening" in this broader sense? Do you know how you might start to change your habits?

You probably know or should know that "hearing" is a smaller part of the communication equation than other factors. Many of you are aware of studies attempting to show the power of nonverbal communication. You can easily find many references to the studies produced some thirty years ago that indicated that only 7 percent of communication was composed of the words used, while 38 percent was the tone of voice with the remaining 55 percent being body language. This is often what leads people to claim that most communication is nonverbal. On the other hand, critics point to the fact that the author himself, in reporting that study, said those percentages only apply when there is inconsistency between tone and actual meaning. But it doesn't really matter what the actual percentages are. What does matter—and you know this well from your own experiences—is that there is a lot going on in communications and settings where they happen.

If you have a significant other, he or she has surely taught you nonverbal communication. Have you been in a group conversation with your partner and others and said "the wrong thing?" Given the social impropriety associated with bickering in front of others, your significant other will sometimes simply give you a look. You don't need words; you know what they mean without them speaking.

Likewise, if you only have written words without nonverbal clues this is challenging as well, confirming the value and importance of a respect for the totality of communication. Do you recall the *Saturday Night Live* episode in which the workers in a nuclear power plant only had a technical manual for guidance after their supervisor had retired? As the plant's nuclear core heated, the workers in the fictional nuclear power plant grabbed the manual to see what they should do. As they looked up the proper procedure in an overheating situation, the solution was water. But the technical manual simply said, "You can't put too much water on the nuclear core." Did this instruction mean the workers should put lots of water on the core? Or did it mean they should be careful not to put too much. After voting, the workers drained the core of water (to avoid "too much water"), the core melted, the plant failed, and the episode ends with an explosion. Had the technical writer spoken the words in person and been available for communication, there would have been no difficulty understanding the right answer.

Those of you who have practiced martial arts in any significant or serious way know that failing to "listen," "pay attention," or be "receptive" means you will get hit.

It's quite possible you will get hurt. As a result, practitioners of martial arts focus keenly in their interactions with others in order to feel or sense what the "opponent" will do next.

Systema, the Russian Martial Arts, offers frequent seminars in Toronto, Ontario, Canada, at its headquarters. I attended one called The Tactics of Confrontation. As Vladmir Vasiliev, one of the co-founders of this European martial art instructed the attendees, he showed us subtle body clues of the opponent that alerted him to what the opponent would do next. "Notice the shoulder that is raised," he would say. "See how his knee is bent," he would point out. There were "hidden clues" that told Vasiliev whether the opponent was going to try to strike with his left or right hand or try to kick. At the time, we thought Vasiliev was simply a genius to notice these subtle clues. But it was teachable genius and while we didn't reach his level in one seminar, we got better. He was listening in this broader sense. He was sensing and we were learning what that meant, and we had to practice those skills.

For the Samurai, these encounters were life or death, not just the possibility of getting hit or hurt. They "listened" in this broader way as they gazed at an opponent. I had an opportunity in Tokyo to confirm this in person during a training session with a razor-sharp sword.

If the Samurai are too far back in history or too esoteric for you, it may be helpful to consider the concept of "The Force" in the ongoing *Star Wars* books and movies. The Force seems to link the physical abilities (lightsaber skills and super powers) with advanced skills interacting with others. Obi-Wan Kenobi tells guards at a checkpoint in the movie *Star Wars Episode IV, A New Hope*, "These aren't the droids you are looking for," and that is the end of it. Obi-Wan persuades the guards with his mind using The Force. It is interesting that the light-sabers of the Jedi resemble the katana of the Samurai. As Ben and then Obi-Wan Kenobi train Luke with respect to the Force, he is told to listen and to feel it. Obi-Wan Kenobi describes the Force as, "An energy field created by all living things." The Force may be stronger in some than others, but it exists in everyone. While *Star Wars* itself never really defines the Force, it was originally named *The Force of Others*. So if you need a metaphor for this broader sense of listening, use the Force. We will work with this broader sense of listening in the chapter on senses.

Notice also that those who train in the Force become and are the leaders. Whether you are Luke, Leia, or Darth Vader, in literature and fiction those with these skills become the leaders. The same is true of those who have mastered the soft skills in our companies and societies. Those individuals who hone these skills will become our leaders.

EXERCISE

1. **Watch a master craftsperson at work.** It can be anything the person does. Watch what he or she does in addition to the simple technical tasks. There are "hidden arts" in all disciplines and you can see them. I watched a worker move the holes in a practice golf green the other day. If I had given you a list of tasks of what to do, you could do it. But this worker also had little tricks, little small things he did. There were hidden arts. He was in touch with his task. The point is for you to become a craftsperson in human interaction so you can understand the little things, the hidden things that generally take many years to learn. This exercise will help you learn to respect the difference between a checklist of tasks and the approach of a craftsman.

2. **Watch a movie.** View one of the original *Star Wars* movies, especially those focusing on the Jedi. Get your own understanding of the Force. Follow Luke, perhaps as he becomes a master at the lightsaber and exercises and refines his instincts. I also encourage you to watch *The Seven Samurai*. I heartily recommend this film but viewing it takes work because it is about

three and a half hours long and is in Japanese (but available with English subtitles).

3. **Watch and listen to a great leader interact with others.** Pick someone you admire for showing leadership or strong values and watch a YouTube video. Chances are you will see an example of that "listening driven" leadership.

SUGGESTED DIALOGUE

You should work to learn how to discern the meaning of various body language and gestures. When someone changes his or her posture as you are speaking, consider stopping speaking. As an example, suppose the person crosses his arms. You may say, "I noticed you crossed your arms, did I say something that bothered you?" If you notice someone giving body language of disapproval, maybe shaking his or her head or looking away, stop and say, "Do you disagree with me; what is your view?" When in doubt about how a conversation is going or how someone is reacting to you, try asking, "What is your opinion? What do you think? How do you feel about what I am saying?"

These suggested dialogues are invaluable. If you know you are potentially running into a roadblock with your listener, more talking won't help. Stop and get the listener talking.

CHAPTER 2

ARE YOU PRESENT? WOODY ALLEN WAS WRONG

"NINETY PERCENT OF life is showing up," Woody Allen said.

Or is it?

Listening is a matter of degrees and a process with many variables. It is definitely not simply an on/off switch. Think about your own listening experiences. Be honest with yourself. You aren't generally listening or not; you are listening "some," perhaps enough to get a portion, a degree, of the speaker's intent. Perhaps you are listening enough to convince the speaker you are listening. Perhaps you are listening to the speaker in accordance with the listening habits you have formed over the years. Perhaps you are listening to the speaker as much as you think he deserves.

If listening were a yes or no or if listening were an on/off switch, all we would need to do is turn it on and then we would have perfect communication. Does that work for you? Can you just say to yourself, "Okay, *this* time I will listen," and then achieve perfect understanding? Sometimes, you might just decide to listen, and if the message is simple and from someone you know well, that will work. But meetings in the workplace, sales calls, negotiations, and other communications in business settings are different. They are substantially more complicated because the interactions are from people with different perspectives, agendas, and feelings, plus we often don't know them nearly as well as we do our family or close personal friends.

Therefore, to become better listeners in the more complex workplace environment, we need to dissect the phases and aspects of listening into parts. Simply showing up to a meeting, sales call, or negotiation is not enough to make you a leader. Leaders don't just show up. Leaders respect the intricacy of work communications. Leaders study the aspects of the communication process. Great leaders learn their constituents' communication styles and use them to their advantage. They know, for example, that Sally likes very explicit communications with great detail and they also know that Michael just needs to be given the general concepts. Leaders know these things because they have developed a framework for learning people. They have gained a framework they use to analyze people and situations.

In this chapter, I give you the framework that I have developed for listening and communicating. I have put it into a phrase that will help you remember and utilize it. The acronym is ARE U PRESENT? This is a fitting acronym because it does several things. First, it reminds us that showing up *does* matter. It reminds us of the most basic requirements of communication—that you are in the moment. But as you learn the acronym, you will remember that being present is not enough and the communication process, for leaders and those who want to be leaders, requires work.

Now, let's examine a framework for better communications. ARE U PRESENT stands for the following:

A = awareness and attention. Is the light on? Is anyone home? This is the showing up aspect of communication. Are you there? Do you have your face in a PDA? Are you reading a newspaper? Are you thinking about things you need to do later? Are you paying attention? While this activity doesn't represent 90 percent of communication, it is hard or even impossible to communicate without it.

R = reception. Are you willing to receive information; are you open? You may be present and aware and even attentive, but your mind may be closed. When your mind is closed you cannot listen and you cannot communicate. Are you willing to learn? Are you willing to change your mind? If you have any bias, how deep is it? If you want to see the opposite of receptivity, watch a political show where each person simply makes his points regardless of what the other side says. These individuals are not receptive and arguably they are not even communicating or having a conversation. You have to be receptive to communicate.

E = engagement. Are you in an interactive state? Is it a fair exchange? Give and take is the key to communications. One of the most fundamental feelings of a human being is the feeling of fairness. Communications require fair exchanges. Good and true communications require a balance between participants. Without balance, we feel cheated. Without give and take, we feel as if something was crammed down our throats. How well does that work in your experience?

U = understanding. Can you interpret what is being said? Do you speak the same language? You can be aware, receptive, and engaged and still lack understanding. Understanding has to do with speaking the same language. Even if I get everything else right, if you are speaking French and I am speaking Italian, we just aren't going to communicate, no matter how fair the exchange is. Understanding requires that you see the other's point of view from their perspective. Understanding is a process of continual "testing" with each person during the course of the conversation.

P = persistence. Do you stay the course? Can you avoid mind drift, distractions, and the interference of your own impressions? Communication, listening, and speaking properly are all work! We view these activities as if they are akin to breathing; that is, they are so natural that they require no thinking or effort. But that is not how leaders view these activities. Leaders are persistent in their communications—they are aware, attentive, receptive, engaged in all the aspects required for great communication, and they maintain those states. Leaders know that the greatest breakthroughs often happen near the end of conversations, and if you don't stick with the discussions, you miss opportunity.

R = resolution. Is there closure to the scenario? Are there takeaways? Are there results that are actionable? Leaders don't view talk as perfunctory. Leaders are doers and are always trying to accomplish more and more. So a leader's conversations, meetings, and interactions are intentional. The leaders are working towards a conclusion that moves their objectives forward. Leaders think about a conversation before they have it and, at the end, assess how it went and whether they accomplished what they wanted. Did they get "buy in?"

E = emotions. How do you feel? How do they feel? How do they make you feel? How does the topic make you and others feel? Leaders respect the existence of emotions and their roles. Emotions can work for you or against you, but it is very important to recognize their roles and learn to discern them. Reread Mark Antony's speech in Shakespeare's play *Julius Caesar* and notice how well he works with emotions in that speech. Leaders are aware of their own emotions and the effect on their ability to "hear" others and communicate with others.

S = senses. Are your other senses of smell, touch, taste, and sight being deployed? Can you sense them and their intent? Leaders bring together the playground and its social training, the gym and its physical training, and the classroom and engage various aspects of our knowledge and background. They bring the entirety of themselves to situations. Great leaders are not one-sided and mono-chromatic. This may be the reason that technical skills are not enough. We need and want the full panoply of a person. Captain Kirk, not Spock, ran the Star Trek *Enterprise*. We yearn for human leadership, not technical leadership.

E = ego. Is your ego tied up in the matter or the people? What is the state of your ego? How is your "I"? In the highly acclaimed business book *Good to Great*, one of the key ingredients to a successful company is a "humble leader." Ego, in this case meaning too much ego, does not correlate with success in business. That's because leading a team means recognizing you are just one person and you are just part of a team. A friend just completed forty successful years with a company he started. When the employees gave him an award and thanked him and recognized him, he said, "I am just one person." This is leadership.

N = nerves. Are you nervous? Are others nervous? Is there tension? Stress is a reality of the workplace. Leaders are able to sense this. Tension gets in the way of productivity. Tension gets in the way of innovation. Stress does not lead to great personal performance. Stress on teams leads to bad judgments and decisions. The workplace is full of stressors such as deadlines, interpersonal conflict, conflicting agendas, enmity, disagreements, and other tensions. Leaders seem to know when to ease tension and when to use it. You can only do this if you are sensitive enough to feel it in the first place. And this means being able to sense and remove your own tensions so you can feel the tension of others.

T = tempo. Are you in touch with the rhythm of the speaker? What is your natural tempo and your timing? Think about what it feels like when the words that are spoken are out of phase with the meaning or out of phase with sight. Have you ever danced, sang, or otherwise performed with someone and you are out of sync? It feels tremendously unnatural and has an effect like that of hearing fingernails scraping on a chalkboard. What is the one quality that leaders—those people who walk in and take over rooms—all have? They are smooth. They have great timing and tempo and most important, they can tailor these qualities for any situation.

Are U Present?

You need to be if you want to be a great leader! As you will see in the coming chapters, "paying attention" is a lot more difficult just looking at the speaker or just showing up. Woody Allen said 90 percent of life is just showing up but he was way off. We are going to explore how to be attentive, receptive, engaging, understanding, persistent, and to reach resolution while paying attention to the senses, emotions, nerves, and tempo of office interactions. We are going to make you a *leader*.

EXERCISE

1. Memorize this mnemonic, putting the abbreviation at key points in your environment and repeat the phrase every morning. I recommend you put the phrase "ARE U PRESENT" somewhere on your desk or maybe post a little sticky note with "ARE U PRESENT" on it. As you work through the book and after you have completed it, use the note as a reminder. Learning the abbreviation and the principles of this book is easy; changing your behavior is extremely challenging.

2. Every morning when you are getting ready for work, take a deep breath (we discuss breathing to get rid of tension later in the book) and say, "I will be present today. I will be aware, receptive, engaged, understanding, persistent, resolved, and in touch with my emotions, senses, ego, nerves, and tempo." You might hit that phrase again before you go to bed to sleep on it. Your brain, as you sleep, will likely review your interactions of the day to measure your adherence to these principles.

SUGGESTED DIALOGUE

You should get in the habit of expanding dialogues to include as many of the principles of ARE U PRESENT as you can. So, the next time you are given an assignment by your boss, try this:

Boss: "Mark, I want you to do some research for me on our competitors and what they are offering as benefits for their employees."

Non-Leader typical responses: "Okay, when do you need it?" or "I am pretty slammed right now, can I have a couple weeks?" A better response would be, "What competitors do you want me to cover? And what benefits?"

Leader-type response: "That sounds like a great assignment! I could do a better assessment if I understand how this would help us. Are we looking to add more benefits? Have we heard that a specific firm has better benefits? Do you think we are spending too much on benefits?" A leader will engage with the manager and get him or her talking. A leader will want to get a sense of the biases or receptivity of the manager to different outcomes. A leader will want to understand the "why" in order to fully understand the assignment.

While it is good to ask about competitors and which benefits are important in order to get a clearer sense of the assignment, these specific points are not crucial. Instead, engaging your manager in a discussion of what is behind the request will put you in a position to deliver the best result. Your manager may think the benefits are fine, but his manager may have just lost a candidate for a job because the applicant heard that a competitor had better benefits. Uncovering the human side of what is going on will help you more capably focus on producing a result and how to go about it. If the reason for the assignment is what is just mentioned, then a survey of employees on how they feel the benefits are compared to where they came from may be more valuable than a simple side-by-side benefits comparison.

CHAPTER 3

AWARENESS AND ATTENTION? MR. MIYAGI WAS WRONG

"Daniel-San, always look eye."

Mr. Miyagi, *The Karate Kid*

DO YOU REMEMBER driver's education class from your high school years? Do you recall learning defensive driving? My experience with defensive driving was working a summer job in a landscaping position; I was part of a team of workers that took care of a utility's power substations that served neighborhoods. We were responsible for cutting grass, pulling weeds, and cleaning up what anyone had left behind at substations in neighborhoods across Omaha. Since I had experience with farm equipment, the managers thought I should be the one to drive the tractor. This sounded great to me, especially compared to pulling weeds and pushing mowers. But before I could drive any equipment for the Omaha Public Power District, I had to complete its defensive driving school. And as you probably experienced as well, the first lesson was called, "Get the Big Picture." We were encouraged not to get a narrow focus on the car in front of us, nor the stoplight up ahead, nor any particular sign. We were taught to take it all in at once. We were to do the opposite of focus, in a way. We were to use our total and peripheral vision.

I had another experience that showed me the importance of focus. I met a former Navy SEAL who lived in Dallas. He was, needless to say, an expert in the use of guns and of defensive shooting tactics, in particular. We agreed that he would train me so I went up to his training facility in North Dallas. We began by working with a training handgun, which shot a laser to check my aim. The object of the training was to point the handgun at a target, which was a black plastic plate that hung on a wall, and then pull the trigger and see where the laser dot hit. I raised the gun to my eye to view the target through the sights, just like you do at a gun range. I felt a slap to the side of my face that I never saw coming. I hadn't seen the instructor. I learned quickly the importance of dropping the gun from my eye and getting the big picture.

Think about the power of a magic show. You are usually astounded at the magician's tricks. That is by design. You can't discern how the magician did most of his tricks, but they all involve distraction. While you focus on one trick, something else is happening. While you look at the scarf, the magician is pulling something out of his cuff. The spectator's inability to get the big picture by focusing only narrowly is the foundation of magic and the key to a magician's ability to surprise you.

These are three good examples of the importance and value of "taking it all in" and getting the big picture. These are lessons for all human encounters. I believe that as a species, in order to survive, humans had to become very adept at getting the big picture. Focusing too much exposes you to vulnerability in another direction. Focusing just on someone's eyes means you miss what the person is doing with his hands, like when you're watching a magician perform. You can't take in body language unless you can see the whole body. Some people gesture a lot, others, not much at all. Some are expressive with their eyes, others, not so much. Getting the big picture means you allow for differences in how people communicate.

Bias Is Blinding

A more serious example of "the big picture" involves the implications of racism and sexism and how these traits impact the ability to understand people. If the color of someone's skin bothers you or catches your attention, if you even care, if you even focus on it, you are missing more important words or behaviors as the person communicates with you. Our reaction and biases to a person's gender, sexual orientation, tattoos and all such perceived differences cause focus on the wrong things. Bias makes a person stupid. Bias works directly against listening and understanding. Someone who is "narrow-minded" is narrowly focused and actually stays in that rut by focusing on the wrong things. Getting the big picture will lead you to be less narrow-minded. This issue is also addressed in Chapter 4 on Receptivity.

The Small Screen Effect

In spite of all the technological advancements in today's world, I think we should ask whether we are moving in the right direction or the wrong direction on "getting the big picture." All indications are that we are moving in the wrong direction. Why? What do we stare at all day? If you're a white-collar employee, chances are you spend your time staring at screens. When you're not spending time looking at the screen, chances are you're viewing some type of handheld device. And that certainly won't give you a big picture!

You can see the value of seeing the big picture and the negative consequences of overly focusing on small screens in a world filled with humans and objects constantly in motion. But our training and our habits, more and more, are on smaller and smaller pictures. The focus on these devices and the limitations flowing from that small focus is so powerful that studies show that the focus on a small object is more of an impairment to driving a motor vehicle than driving while impaired from alcohol.

The Opposite of "Attention and Awareness" Is Distraction

We have given dignity to the act of being distracted. We call it "multitasking" and that makes it sound like an achievement. Multitasking sounds like something perhaps a new superhero does. But we now know from studies that in fact multitasking is associated with fatal car accidents, and multitasking does *not*, in fact, produce superior results.

Before there were handheld devices and the internet, a lot of news came through newspapers and magazines. Nobody would have thought it acceptable behavior to open a newspaper or magazine in the middle of a conversation. But it is not unusual now, is it? Haven't you been in meetings where people have their face in their device?

The importance of getting the big picture is not a new idea. Keeping your mind aware and moving about was captured beautifully in this passage from the ancient book *The Unfettered Mind: Writings from a Zen Master to a Master Swordsman*, which is about a samurai teacher, Tajuan Soho (1573–1645) training his student, Yagyu Munenori, a rival to Miyamoto Musashi (author of *The*

Book of Five Rings), in Japanese swordsmanship. Read the following passage:

> The Right Mind is the mind that does not remain in one place. It is the mind that stretches throughout the entire body and self.
>
> The Confused Mind is the mind that, thinking something over, congeals in one place.
>
> When the Right Mind congeals and settles in one place, it becomes what is called the Confused Mind. When the Right Mind is lost, it is lacking in function here and there. For this reason, it is important not to lose it.
>
> In not remaining in one place, the Right Mind is like water. The Confused Mind is like ice, and ice is unable to wash hands or head. When ice is melted, it becomes water and flows everywhere, and it can wash the hands, the feet, or anything else.
>
> If the mind congeals in one place and remains with one thing, it is like frozen water and is unable to be used freely: ice that can wash neither hands nor feet. When the mind is melted and is used like water, extending throughout the body, it can be sent wherever one wants to send it.
>
> That is the Right Mind.

EXERCISE

1. **Exercise your peripheral vision.** Some people
    have set alarms for their phones alerting them
    when to get up and when to exercise. One of
    my apps tells me to drink water periodically.
    If you have one of those programs, use it as a
    reminder to step back from your devices and
    get a big gulp of vision. If you have to leave
    your desk, leave your desk. If you even have
    to leave your office, leave your office. But find
    some scene where you can take in a big picture.
    If you watch TV while you exercise, expand
    your vision. Look at the TV as just part of the
    scene. What else is there in your surround-
    ings? Exercise your vision by using your finger
    in front of your face and move it inwards and
    outwards. Focus only on your finger and then
    gradually expand your view as you move your
    finger from your face outwards. If something is
    moving in your field of vision, don't get stuck
    on it. Don't dwell on it or any single object,
    simply be aware of it and keep moving.

2. **When you are in a meeting or listening to
    someone speak, pay attention to the speaker.**
    But use the previous exercises to expand your
    field of vision so you can take in how others
    are reacting to her or him. Move from person

to person while keeping the speaker in your gaze as well. When "talking heads" are on CNN or one of the other news channels, don't just look at the person speaking. Train yourself to observe others' reactions, including the hosts to the speaker. Think like the person who directs the cameras and take lots of shots from multiple perspectives.

3. **Train yourself by watching professionals.** Look for professionals who are trained to "get the big picture." At public events where there are politicians or other public figures requiring security, there are Secret Service or private security at the venue. A trained observer will note that these specialists' eyes are not fixed, but rather they roam back and forth as they take in whatever "landscape" is within their responsibility. Look for people like that, and then practice doing what you see them do.

SUGGESTED DIALOGUE

At your next meeting with multiple participants, let your gaze wander from person to person and watch their reactions while you take in the speaker's comments as well. If you notice a reaction that is negative, aloof, or not positive, interject at the appropriate time and say, "Jane, can you repeat what you just said in a different way? I am sorry, I am having a little trouble following it." The others will sincerely appreciate you doing this and you will improve the communication for everyone.

In your next sales call pay attention to the surroundings of the office of the person to whom you are selling and pay attention to what the person is wearing. If, for example, you see a sports poster in the office, you will want to observe something like, "Are you a San Francisco Giants fan?" Make sure you make it a question because there is a story behind everything in someone's office. That is why it is there after all—it has some meaning for the person. But don't presume the meaning; ask about it.

CHAPTER 4

CHAPTER 4

ARE YOU RECEPTIVE? OR ARE YOUR "SHIELDS UP?"

ARE YOU OPEN to any messages? Have you learned to change your mind? Are you aware of your bias?

Don't Talk to Strangers: Shields Up!

What is one of the first things you are told by your parents as a child? Strangers are scary people and not to be trusted or engaged. Maybe this is one reason why cold calling is so intimidating, do you suppose? By definition, you are calling a stranger.

Do you recall the 1960s television program *Star Trek*? The original show had wonderful characters like William Shatner's James T. Kirk. An unknown threat in a faraway galaxy would present itself to sensors monitored by Sulu. Kirk would ask that it be placed on the big screen on the command center they called "the bridge." Sulu wouldn't be able to identify it. Lieutenant Ohura would try, unsuccessfully, to communicate with it via any known languages. Often, even Spock would be stumped and wouldn't speculate because he couldn't be certain. What next? Captain Kirk would order "Shields up!" "Shields up" was a defense mechanism and prevented anything from getting through. And, if necessary "red alert." Battle stations!

How often do we approach an interaction in our lives and in the work place with "shields up"? What are the consequences? What causes "shields up"?

How to Recognize "Shields Up"

You are speaking to someone, perhaps several people. As you say something, you see their faces change and their lips begin to move. You should know they have stopped listening to you. You should know they have already formulated their position and they are going to respond. But you are still talking. You may find yourself saying, "Wait, I am not finished." After they interrupt you and make what they think will be your point for you, you may find yourself saying, "That's not what I was going to say." When you saw their faces change, they stopped listening to you. Their shields went up.

Body language is a real key to signaling when someone is and is not receptive to you. People who *are* receptive, *act* receptive. People who aren't receptive know how to show it. All you need to do is to pay attention. Receptive folks have open arms, not crossed arms. Receptive folks nod and smile. Nonreceptive folks shake their heads and frown. People are showing you how receptive they are, but you need to be aware and getting the big picture to see it and be trained to feel it. Closed-minded people actually show you they are closed for business.

Besides body language, people use intonation and word selection to demonstrate their closed mind on a topic. The tone of someone's voice is a key giveaway to receptivity. People will raise their voice when they are not receptive. Also, they will speak in absolute and over-stated terms in opposition. Words like "never" and other extremes are ways we express closed mindedness.

Emotions and Receptivity

While we will discuss the role of emotions in a later chapter dedicated to the subject, emotions play a key role in someone's receptivity to information.

You may be speaking to someone who has an emotional reaction to what you say. Communications with children often invoke emotional reactions. "Dad, can I go to Jack's lake house?" Shields up! You immediately become emotional because you are worried, based upon what you have heard about Jack's lake house and what goes on there. You are thinking that there will be drinking by underage kids, that they will do something stupid, including driving while drunk, and someone, potentially your son or daughter, will get hurt. Your shields go up! You are not receptive and you show it with your physical reaction and your tone of voice.

In all of these situations, someone in the communication has ceased being receptive. He or she is aware and may even be getting the big picture. But the person is not in a position to be receptive and open and your thoughts are not accepted or appreciated.

Bias Gets in the Way

Race, gender, sexual orientation, religion, and other biases already discussed can also cause people to be nonreceptive. When you encounter someone against whom you are biased, you will not be receptive to what the individual has to say.

Your own self and your ego can be a major cause of nonreceptiveness. (This important topic is explored in detail in Chapter 11 on Ego.)

Everyone has someone or several people in their lives who annoy them when they talk. You want to listen, but maybe their tone of voice or their opinion bothers you. Maybe you're just bothered by the person. Whatever it is, when something annoys you enough that your temper rises and you get riled up, try to start a new conversation or possibly just walk away altogether. The extremes are easy to recognize. What is harder to recognize is that there is a little bit of reaction to everyone when they speak. You bring yourself into every encounter, and that's a big problem.

The willingness and ability to receive is affected greatly by these reactions. Is the speaker friend or foe? Do you regularly disagree or agree with him or her? Do you have some bias against people with this position, race, color, ethnicity, religion, physical characteristics, or even their name?

It was 1987 and I had just been promoted out of the law department of the Union Pacific Railroad where I was a corporate attorney focusing on mergers and acquisitions. My new job was general manager of the air-freight division that had been acquired with the merger of the Missouri Pacific Railroad. I was in my twenties, and the employees I would be managing in the St. Louis operation were much older, in many cases double my age, and they all had a lot more experience. I had spent a few years doing deals in the corporate law department and had not managed anyone yet. I had nearly completed my MBA, but I hadn't supervised or led any type of major project. What do sophisticated companies do with young novices like I was in such a situation? They send you to leadership school!

So off I went to The Center for Creative Leadership that was being held at that time in St. Petersburg, Florida, at Eckerd College. It was an outstanding experience that I will never forget; we integrated with others who were headed back to new leadership positions. There were executives from Kroger, the FBI, an accountant from the Kingdom of Saudi Arabia, and many others from all over the world. There were about twenty of us. I would like to tell you their names, but I can't. Their names weren't classified or anything, but we never knew each other's names. You have to wonder, as I did at the time, why the names were withheld and never disclosed.

As we learned, we tend to discriminate against people based upon their names. In some deep way, if your name is Stacy, I form an immediate impression of you as some amalgam, some combination, of every Stacy I have met. As a result, I probably view you as someone quite different from who you actually are. I react to you differently. I "hear" you differently. To eliminate this "bias" during leadership school, attendees were only given a Greek letter as a name. For example, suppose your name was Frank. For the duration of the Center for Creative Leadership program Frank's name was "Omega." When you consider that something as small as someone's name led to bias, imagine all of the rest of the hurdles we face in being purely receptive to other people, their ideas, and their thoughts.

Whenever people doubt me about the power and impact of names on our psyche, I like to tell them the story about my family's move from Chicago to San Francisco in the mid-90s. I had been offered a crisis consulting position in San Francisco for a company that was in bankruptcy in a field I understood very well. As my father was ill with cancer in San Diego, I wanted to be closer to him so our young children could get to know him better. I was commuting back and forth and looking at homes while I was in the Bay Area. I had settled upon a charming bedroom community in the East Bay and a neighborhood known as Happy Valley. The elementary school was even called Happy Valley School. I would update my children, who were of elementary school age, on the progress of the search, and, although having the usual fear and trepidation about relocating, they loved the sound of Happy Valley. As I was bidding on the house in that neighborhood, the deal went south and my search refocused on another neighborhood on another potential deal. When I returned to Chicago and gave my update on the home search, all three of them cried. "We wanted to live in Happy Valley," they all said in tears. None of them had ever seen Happy Valley and knew nothing but its name. But they were not receptive to any neighborhood other than Happy Valley. They were drawn to the name and it affected their view dramatically.

A comprehensive list of all bias is not possible in this book. But common ones are worth discussing. Physical appearance is a strong bias. Study after study shows that better-looking people succeed more. Better-looking lawyers get more successful results and make more money. Taller folks win elections. There's even a reliable algorithm on who would be elected in a contested political contest simply based on his or her pictures on a poster. Racial bias, obesity bias, color of hair bias, gender bias, age bias, and color of skin bias are just some of these physical biases. Even those of us who think we are pure from these perspectives probably aren't. Have you, as a white person, ever said, "I need to be extra attentive to listen to this person as he or she is a minority"? Maybe that is a good thing, but the consciousness of it by itself shows there is a bias.

We also have bias against certain behaviors. We may be biased against sexual orientation that we perceive. We may be biased against aggressive people or shy people. This can be very subtle. When I was at the leadership school, I learned that I had bias against the introverted. How did I discover this? A psychologist and a fellow participant pointed this out to me. At the end of the weeklong training, we debriefed with psychologists who had observed our every move during the training. We also were responsible for observing a peer and a peer was responsible for observing us for feedback purposes. One of the peers who sat in with me on my debrief session I remembered well as someone who didn't help much in our various exercises we did together. Those exercises consisted of group activities like being stranded on the moon and having to decide what items to take with us from our damaged shuttle to take to another potential rescue spot. The peer in question, I never knew his name, didn't help us at all; he didn't say a word. It was frustrating. So what happened next was interesting. In my review, the psychologist said I discriminated against introverts!

Me, I was the problem? The peer followed up and said I wasn't as nice to him as he would have expected from the leader of the group. I said to the peer, "I'm sorry you didn't think I was nice, but we did three survival exercises and two projects together and you said and did nothing." He looked at me like I was crazy and said, "You never asked me what I thought." I was stunned. But I learned that final day at the end of the week that I was biased in favor of the extroverts and against introverts. I learned that if you aren't communicating with an extrovert, you aren't listening and if you aren't communicating well with an introvert you aren't asking. In other words, the process of listening to an introvert includes *asking*!

The tone of people's voices affects how and what we hear. This is why radio and TV stations hire those "voices." This is why commercials hire "voice" experts. This is why Bruce Buffer is the UFC announcer. Tone matters. The more pleasing the voice, the more we take in the message coming from it. The more shrill or painful, the less enjoyable and the less we willingly digest. It just isn't tone, it is also volume.

There are an infinite number of factors that can make you not receptive to another person. What is important, however, is not the infinite factors, but yours.

How can you find what is making you less receptive in order to open yourself up to learning and advancement? Try the following exercises.

EXERCISE

1. **Spend some quiet time thinking about people who annoy you.** Think about people you don't like. Write down their names (remember to throw this away when you are done!). What don't you like? What caused you to stop liking them? What annoys you about them? Now, as rational as you may feel about not liking these people, they are important to you because who or what you don't like shows you have a bias and that something is holding you back. The very trait that you associate with someone you don't like will cause you to dislike anyone with that trait. And, as we implicitly learned at Leadership School when I was young, this will cause you not to like other people with that trait or even those who have the same name. Understanding this reflection will help you greatly reduce your bias towards others.

2. **Reflect on your likes and dislikes in an explicit way.** This second exercise is more dynamic and is a skill you must practice, practice,

and practice. It will take you some time and reading the rest of the book to be in touch with your feelings and reactions towards others to analyze why you feel a particular way around certain other people. Admit this, when you meet someone and you immediately form an impression. It is often thought that juries form opinions about defendants in the first thirty seconds. A more recent study claimed we form opinions about others in milliseconds. If you don't understand the "hidden arts" of inter-personal relationships, then you won't form better impressions and people will form the wrong impression of you. Working on this skill is at the heart of what will change your life. Specific instructions can be found in Chapter 19, "Your 90 Day Listening Improvement Plan." For now, after you meet someone new, reflect on your likes and dislikes in an explicit way. This process will help you with further engagements with the individual and with others.

3. **Try an exercise by tensing your most tense body part as you inhale and relax it as you exhale.** When you practice martial arts at the higher levels, you become aware of your tension and your breathing. In Systema, the Russian Martial Arts practice, practitioners practice segmented tension breathing

exercises to get in touch with their internal issues so they are aware of their tension. These exercises, described more fully in Chapter 12, "Nerves and Tension," clean you up and get you out of the way of your tension and stress so you can be more responsive. Literally speaking, you can't feel someone else if you are full of tension yourself. Try a segmented tension exercise by tensing your most tense body part as you inhale and relax it as you exhale. Some people carry tension in their neck, some in their gut, and some in their back. We grow accustomed to the feeling of tension and thus it begins to feel normal. Segmented tension exercises will show you that this is not a normal feeling and help you with a method to remedy the tension.

SUGGESTED DIALOGUE

When someone gives you negative feedback, e.g., crossed arms, frown, and change of face that is not positive—stop talking! Instead say, "I'm sorry, are we on the same page or did I lose you?" You can keep talking, but why bother? All you will do is drive a deeper divide that you may not recover from. Sincerity and honesty is best here; just say it like it feels. "Suzie, I sense you are not agreeing with what I am saying, where did we part ways?" Or, "John, I am going to stop here because I think you have something to say." All of these statements make it more likely that you will have a meaningful conversation and interaction whether it involves a sales call, group company meeting, or face-to-face interview.

CHAPTER 5

ENGAGEMENT AND GIVE AND TAKE

ARE YOU GIVING *and* receiving? Is there a fair exchange?

The role of a training partner is an important aspect of martial arts training. In all martial arts, the student and his or her training partner take turns giving and receiving attacks. In a training exercise, you learn both by giving and receiving strikes and by being offensive and defensive. It would be unimaginable and unthinkable to have a training session where the word "*switch*" wasn't uttered. An instructor shouting the word "*switch*" is your cue to change roles. You now defend if you were the attacking training partner and you attack if you were the defending training partner. Think of it this way, since attacking may involve striking your opponent, how fair would it be if you only got hit? Likewise, what would you learn about defending yourself if you only did the striking?

Great conversations involve give and take. Great sales calls involve give and take. Great interviews involve give and take. There is nothing more annoying and unsuccessful than a salesperson who can't shut up. There is no worse interview than one in which the candidate or the interviewer does all the talking. The worst and most unproductive meetings involve someone dominating the conversation to the exclusion of others. All human advancement involving more than one person is the result of a fair, balanced, and bargained exchange of information between them.

In order to understand the concept and value of engagement and a fair, balanced, and bargained exchange of information, let's look at the opposite. What is the worst example of communication? That's obvious: it's a knock-down, drag out argument—a disagreement of major proportions. By now, you should have a framework for and understand why an argument doesn't change someone's opinion, and why everyone walks away mad.

It doesn't start with an argument. Arguments often arise out of civil conversations. Reflect on a recent argument you have been a part of or witnessed. What caused it? Break it down. Did the "shields go up"? Receptivity ended. Engagement ensued, but there was no give and take, just give and give from one followed by give and give from the other.

You have been a part of great conversations in your life. You have danced in your life. If you're trained in the martial arts, you have experienced some great training sessions. All of these events are characterized by a rhythmic exchange. They don't feel clunky—they feel natural. You breathe and move. When this occurs, you get in the moment. And in that moment, you share, you learn, you remember, and you both advance. It's beautiful.

Fairness is one of the earliest concepts we understand as children. If you don't remember your own childhood, observe your children. If your children are older, observe their children. The phases of childhood development are fascinating to observe, especially when a toddler enjoys saying "no" to everything. It is an exercise of will that is part of growing up.

All of you have undoubtedly uttered the phrase, "That is not fair," at some point. Fairness matters, at home, in relationships, and of course in the workplace. It is the basis of many employee issues. You did something improper in early school education, for example, and you got punished. If someone else did the same thing and got a lighter punishment your reaction was swift to declare it unfair!

The give and take of a great conversation requires fairness. If someone feels unfairly treated, you will have a very hard time getting through to him or her on any issue. They will never like or respect you as much as you want or as much as they could, or maybe should.

Interrupting someone is unfair, isn't it? When someone interrupts you the first thing you feel is that someone has broken a rule of fairness and crossed a line they are not supposed to cross. Interrupting someone is an act of selfishness. They may even apologize as they do it: *I Am Sorry to Interrupt You, But...*

You just don't want to hear it.

Give and take in a good conversation takes an incredible amount of patience. What happens when we become impatient? We interrupt the speakers—those who are trying to express themselves. Of all the difficulties involved in effective listening, especially between those who work together or are in a more intimate relationship, interrupting one another is the most damaging. What is the cost of dysfunctional communication? The result is suboptimal performance in a team, and emotional side effects and scars that lead to even worse performance over the long term. If the interruption happens in an intimate relationship, it can permanently impair your interactions with your partner, friend, or child.

How can you stop, or at least reduce, your tendency to interrupt others? It happens so fast. And what do interrupters (including myself) say? "I'm sorry, I didn't mean to interrupt." Or, "I am sorry to interrupt you, but..." Think about those phrases. Of course, you didn't *mean* to interrupt, but you did. Are you or they really sorry to interrupt? You may be sorry to have to do it, but not sorry you did it. There is a difference.

Some folks, especially those who repeatedly interrupt, do so in a way that makes it seem impulsive; almost like an involuntary act? Whether you are the perpetrator of an interruption or the victim, it happens so fast, doesn't it? Because this can become an impulsive habit, if you want to interrupt less, you have to understand the root causes of interrupting, and that interrupting someone comes at the end of a process.

To help you understand the root causes of the interrupting process, I identify and describe various types of "talkers" and "listeners" and their traits. Your ability to recognize these types will enable you to react in a more productive manner. In the exercises at the end of this chapter, you'll find tips and practice exercises to help you avoid interrupting and to reduce the likelihood that you will be interrupted.

The Talkers

The Slow Talker—Someone is talking and he or she just isn't going fast enough; you have to get the person talking faster. You feel the need to nudge the person along so you can catch a plane, a train, get home, get other work done, or do whatever is driving your schedule that day.

The Rambler—Someone is making a pointless speech. Think John Candy in *Planes, Trains and Automobiles*. This is talking that seemingly has no beginning, no end, and therefore absolutely no point whatsoever. When the speech is over, nobody knows what to do or to say. When this happens in a group setting, everyone will tend to look around at one another dumbfounded.

The Repeater—This is the person who seems to repeat things that have already been said. You have already heard the point being made, so who needs it? When Repeaters say something that has already been said, they could be practicing active listening to themselves. Or perhaps they are just absorbing the content for the first time. People absorb ideas at such varying rates and in very different ways. Some people think conceptually and they get it fast. Other people are engineers who need to see the bricks in place more than once. Is one listening style or speed better than the other? Of course not. Once engineers "see the bricks," they tend to have a deeper understanding than the fast-moving, conceptual thinker.

The Listeners

The Conversation "Dominator"—This is the person who is constantly interrupting others and dominating the conversation. Taking on this person leads to a conversational brawl.

The "You Are Wrong"—This interrupter disagrees with you so he needs to correct you, and the sooner the better. This is a special category of mistake. If you interrupt people you disagree with, you may end up with a "group-think" level of decision-making. In other words, you are so set in your ways and opinion that you lose the possibility—no matter how slight you think that is—of learning something. (For more insights on "group-think" read some articles about "group think.") Basically, "group think" is a label of social psychology that is identified when the group consciously favors consensus over contrary opinion. Very bad judgments can occur as a result. In one of the original books on the subject, *Groupthink, A Psychological Study of Policy Decisions and Fiascos*, author Irving Janis used the failed Bay of Pigs invasion and Pearl Harbor as examples of disasters that flowed from "group think."

The "You Are Stupid; I Am Superior to You"—These interrupters think they are smarter, more successful, have higher social status, and are better looking than everyone else. They feel entitled to interrupt anyone to whom they feel superior in some respect. If you are this type of person, your "superiority" will be short lived. Eventually, nobody will listen to you. You should acquire some humility by spending time with people who are smarter, more successful, have higher social status, or are better looking than you. If you can't find someone superior to yourself, you have serious problems that may require professional assistance.

The "I Already Know What You Are Going to Say"—The person with this trait is probably someone with whom you're very familiar based on years of interactions.

If you're the person who always seems to be interrupted, then you should look for reasons why. Do you recognize yourself in any of the aforementioned types of talkers?

Conversations that include interruptions, whatever the root cause, become choppy and convoluted, and no participants are able to express themselves fully. Instead, the conversation is like a competitive sports match where the umpire or referee is constantly stopping the action. Pick your combat sport. A conversation full of interruption is like a bad boxing or wrestling match full of punches and counterpunches with inopportune stops that destroy its beauty and flow. Interrupting facilitates arguments and disagreements because no one gets the chance to complete a thought; moreover, negative emotions come into play like anger, anxiety, and even depression. Do you reach better solutions or consensus with incomplete thoughts and interruptions? Tell me the last time you changed someone's mind during an argument or "competitive conversation." You can't think of a situation because competitive conversation doesn't work. Combative conversation does not progress thinking and decision-making. All it does is feed the egos of the combatants. And as you probably have noticed, combative conversation becomes physical very quickly. Participants raise their voices. Combatants "square off." Blood pressures rise and nostrils flare. Tones and volumes increase. All of the elements discussed in this book go out the window. Listening? *Gone.*

Interrupting is the ultimate arrogant and selfish act. Learning not to interrupt someone is part of a child's preschool or kindergarten education. It is a lesson as valuable as taking turns and learning to share. These are some of the earliest lessons we probably remember. We know better. And if you fix this trait, as with any positive change in behavior, there will be a positive halo effect on other behaviors you have. Interrupt less and you are likely to be generally less rude and less aggressive, and will learn more from those around you. Pay attention to these root causes and watch out for them before they become habitual and hurt you, personally or professionally. And if you find yourself interrupted often, check yourself for the root causes. If you can think of interrupting as the equivalent of banging the bottom of an old ketchup bottle, then you understand how the victims of interrupting feel. Great listening, like great ketchup, is worth the wait.

EXERCISE

1. **Pick someone you know to be a slow talker and engage with him or her.** Don't try to nudge the individual along. The person could be an introvert. Breathe and give him or her the time to develop and express his or her thoughts. Remember the parable of the tortoise and the hare. This person may be the tortoise, who actually wins the race. And when you engage with the person, slow down yourself. This is a very effective sales and communication strategy: matching speech patterns.

2. **Pick someone you have known for a long time, and engage them in conversation.** They could be a spouse, significant other, a long-term coworker, or a relative. Before you engage with this person, write down some phrases related to what you *think* about the person. What biases do you have towards him? What preconceived notions do you have of him? These biases and preconceived notions lead us to literally substitute what we think he will say for what he may say. You are also more likely to interrupt him, because, after all, why wait for what you know is coming? This is what I refer to as the Presumptive Interruption. This exercise will enable you to be consciously aware of your

desires to interrupt and why. Stop presuming that you know where someone's thoughts are headed. Thoughts are actually very personal and can change day to day and hour to hour based upon someone's feelings, attitudes, and emotions. Calm yourself and empty your mind of preconceptions. Listen openly.

3. **As painful as it might be, engage in a conversation with someone you believe to be a Rambler or Dominator.** Ramblers and Dominators are the hardest folks to handle when it comes to conversation and listening. With Ramblers, try some body language feedback for this incessant talker. You might look at your watch or fidget. Look away or into the distance. Here you are breaking the rules of listening to get the attention of the speaker, so you basically are doing the *opposite* of what you should to try to "train" the speaker. Most communication is nonverbal. Work that. Alternatively, or in addition, at an appropriate time you can explain your time limitation. By "appropriate time" I mean when you can interject without interrupting. There is nothing wrong with saying you have a commitment in a few minutes. Another strategy is to let the speaker know in advance that you only have "X" minutes. This

can be the least offensive and most effective technique to limit rambling.

4. **Learn to manage the Dominator.** We sometimes act like as if there is only one way to prevent this, by avoiding Dominators. But what if they are on your team or a team leader? Find a time outside of the conversation to discuss this issue with the Dominator. If you are the team leader, or even if you are a key influencer, you can use some group techniques that will ensure you smooth their dominance. Here are a couple of facilitating techniques that should be effective at handling a Dominator. In a meeting, go around the room in round-robin fashion to solicit input so one person doesn't dominate. Just start from the left or right and go around the room. Another easy tactic is to announce that you, or the group, will only take input from those who have not yet contributed. Practice those techniques when you are put in a position of leadership or have the influence necessary to do so.

SUGGESTED DIALOGUE

Don't change the subject to what you want to talk about when you are engaged with someone. An interviewer says, "Sorry, I am running behind and that you had to wait." You could say, "Thanks for your time, I really think I am qualified for this position because of X, Y, and Z." You want to get to the meat of why you are qualified. You want to "sell" them. But a more effective response would be, "I am sure it is a busy day with all the interviews, how do you keep them straight?" I like this response better because it accomplishes several things. First, it shows that you are sympathetic to the interviewer's day and his responsibilities. Second, you are complimenting the person for his ability to keep everything together. But what I really like is that this line gives you a chance to learn about how the interviewer views interviews and what he notices. Understanding this might help you in your responses. Meet people where they are. Give and take on their subject, don't change to yours.

Sales calls are the same way. We are so anxious to "sell" someone our product or service that we lose them at the starting line. Get a good "give and take" conversation going and the person you're selling to will form an immediate positive impression of you. You don't have to make some clumsy attempt to establish a common interest. Just engage in give and take. If the person says he is having a crazy day, then you talk about that. "It has been a crazy day," says your prospect. Don't say, "I have crazy days too." Say, "What is a crazy day like at Company A?" Get the individual talking about whatever he cares about. The person doesn't care about your problems; he cares about his. Get over yourself and engage with the person.

CHAPTER 6

UNDERSTANDING? PERSPECTIVE LISTENING AND CONFIRMING UNDERSTANDING

CAN YOU SEE the world from the speaker's perspective? Are you sure you understand what he or she means?

Let's assume you have done a good job at being aware. You are getting the Big Picture. You have identified your biases and your antennae are prepared to keep your biases in check so that you get a warning signal when they surface in a conversation. You are also having an excellent give and take with a prospect, interviewer, candidate, coworker, or other person with whom you are communicating.

The next challenge is taking in the packets of information that the speaker intends so the conversation is not perfunctory and you avoid misunderstanding. There are two aspects of understanding that will be examined in this chapter. The first is confirming understanding as you are engaged with a person. Engaging in give and take, as discussed in the last chapter, is one form of active listening. Active listening is generally defined as listening that is not passive but rather engaged in working to understand another, often including paraphrasing and repeating what a speaker says. Active listening includes confirming understanding. I cover active listening in this chapter. A second aspect of understanding another is working yourself into the speaker's world; you need to put yourself in the speaker's shoes.

Confirming understanding is crucial to any great conversation or exchange. The act of confirming understanding is by its nature an affirmation of the other person. If you say to me, "I get what you are saying," you are giving me a verbal hug. You are reinforcing me. You are telling me, "I get it."

In martial arts training, there is a lot of confirmation of understanding. In a typical training exercise, one person is the aggressor and one is the receiver. The aggressor will initiate an attack and the defender or receiver will execute a technique that he has been taught. For example, the aggressor will perform a straight punch and the receiver will execute a block and a counterpunch. The two training partners will do this over and over again. They will confirm with each other after each trial by saying, "Did I get that right?" or "How was that?" These iterations are performed repeatedly and the confirmations are continuous. This is how martial arts techniques are "burned in."

We rely on muscle memory in the traditional martial arts, which results from focus, concentration, and repeated practice over time. We then confirm all of this on a continuous basis with our training partner. Imagine a great conversation or interview that has that give and take with constant adjustment to ensure understanding. Now picture the rhythm of the training partners. Don't worry about mastering fancy tactics to remember what is said; you will "burn the content in."

Another approach to understanding, besides "active listening," is what I call "perspective listening." When someone is speaking, his meaning is tied up with his perspective. The best way to think of this level of understanding is to imagine walking in the shoes of the person with whom you are speaking and communicating. Understanding at this level involves seeing the world from someone else's point of view. This can be very difficult, especially if you disagree with the person. But you need to do it *especially* if you disagree with the person.

If you want to understand how a person feels, what is the best way to do it? In Brazilian Jiu Jitsu, which is a martial art that to the common eye would look like wrestling or grappling, we work from positions on our back or on top or to the side of someone. There are techniques that cause pain that you would use in an actual confrontation. These are called submissions. Since we don't want to hurt someone during training, we apply pressure until they "tap out." You literally tap the other person so he knows you have had enough. It is very important that you feel the pain that you want to be able to inflict. These submissions often involve the physics of the body. The techniques work due to the angle of pressure that is beyond the design of a joint. Until you feel the pain itself, you can't apply the technique, the submission, yourself. You have to literally become the "victim" in order to successfully learn how to be the person applying the hold. This is true of every submission and most techniques in Brazilian Jiu Jitsu.

In understanding at this level, you hear nothing but questions in good exchanges. "Is this right?" or "Can you feel that?" Great understanding comes from this level of exchange. "Perspective Listening" requires you literally to get to the other person's point of view. You need to feel what it is like to understand the perspective of the person across from you in a conversation, interview, or meeting.

For those in sales, which we cover in Chapter 16 "Listening and Selling," this means, among other things, knowing the role of the person or people with whom you are engaged. You need to know their perspective. If they work in procurement, they care about price. If they work in a team that is trying to build a car or airplane, they care more about your part or service quality and reliability. You have to know their role in order to know their perspective.

But their "role" is just one factor as an example. For Perspective Listening, you need to differentiate this person from other people. What makes someone Jonathan? Can you sense what someone thinks that makes them Jonathan? For this, you need to exercise your observational powers. People are telling you loudly who they are and what they care about from how they act and how they appear. Are they more external or internal? Are they dressed meticulously or casually? Are they heavily accessorized? What is their purse or wallet like? How about their shoes? Are they careful in their speech? Where are they from? There is so much you can see and hear that can help you with that person's perspective. Did they graduate from college? Where?

Everyone is unique and the more you can get to understand and know them, the better your exchanges of information will be. I often have to remind people when explaining this that there are roughly 7 billion people in the world and each has a unique set of fingerprints! It is part of your responsibility as a human who wants to exchange with others to understand the other's point of view and perspective.

The other aspect of this chapter, confirming understanding, is a primary tool to help you learn the perspective of the other person. Mastering these two tools—Perspective Listening and confirming understanding—can turn you into an incredible conversationalist.

EXERCISE

1. **In your conversations or exchanges for the next week, limit yourself to questions only.** To learn to confirm understanding, you need to be comfortable asking many, many questions. You need to get better at asking questions *by asking questions*. If this seems too awkward or difficult for you, then make as few statements as possible so that the vast majority of what you say in the conversation or meeting are questions. Once a month, try doing this for a week's duration. Returning consciously to this technique will bring it into your habitual behavior.

2. **Get a conversation partner, someone who will practice with you.** It would be ideal if the person was very different than you so you will acquire a dissimilar perspective. If you are a woman, choose a man as your conversation partner. If you are young, find someone older. If you are white, go with someone from

a different race or ethnicity. If you are straight, pick an LGBTQ friend. See a movie together and then discuss it in a structured way. Try to pick a movie that emphasizes differences. Maybe use the following questions or something like them: What was the point of the movie? Who was the character you identified with the most? The least? What other movie that you have seen was it most similar to? Would you recommend it to others? If so, how would you describe it?

As you ask each other these questions, continually work to understand the other person's point of view. Try to understand how his perspective plays a role in how he talks about the film. When you have a difference of opinion, make sure there is a constant back and forth and ask questions until you understand the perspective of your conversation partner.

SUGGESTED DIALOGUE

The biggest mistake when attempting to confirm understanding is becoming a repeater or a "reporter" and being perfunctory about it. Someone says to you, "I don't think that our approach to client A will be successful, I think we need to lower our price." You may say back, "So you think we should lower our price?" You have to and can do better than that. What the person is saying to you in that one sentence isn't just that the price is too high. The person is questioning the value to the customer of whatever it is you are selling. Do justice to everything someone says. A better response from you would be, "What part of our approach do you think needs improving?" The statement that "we need to lower our price" is a conclusion. You may get to that conclusion, but you should first examine the person's overall issues with the "approach."

In sum, in your dialogues, try to avoid confirming conclusions and examine uncertainties.

CHAPTER 7

PERSISTENCE– CAN YOU STAY IN THE GAME?

AS I SAID at the beginning of this book, when you consider listening (including your own habits as well as your observations of others), you will recognize that listening is not an on-and-off switch. We generally are not either listening or not listening. Sometimes we are tuning in and out and only getting pieces. We recognize this when we say to someone listening to us: "I am not sure you got that part." It is not unusual to remember the beginning or the end of something because that is what we "heard" the most. Ever hear someone say, "What was the middle part again?" Listening is more a matter of degree. If your spouse is sharing something really important with you, you may be listening at a very high level. On the other hand, a friend may be talking about something you're not interested in and you realize that you checked out. We all check out now and then. In fact, if we are honest with ourselves, most of the time we are only partially listening. Whether you are simply checked out or you are only partially listening, you certainly are not attaining the level of understanding you could have nor will you remember as much of the content as you should.

You know the feeling. You have felt it. It is a sinking feeling followed by panic. Someone is talking to you and your mind has drifted. And then the person says, "What do you think?" And you think, but don't say, "About what?" Yikes! Whether a cellphone or your Blackberry distracts you, your own thoughts on the subject being discussed, or you just get plain bored, mind drifting happens. Let's face it. It's challenging to quiet your mind completely. Why? Because the human mind has been designed and evolved to be "ready." A ready mind is active, and active minds tend to wander. In fact, it's likely that there's an evolutionary reason our minds are active. There were so many threats our ancestors faced, their brains had to be constantly vigilant and move from threat to threat. How should you handle drifting off in the middle of a conversation and can you reduce "drift" in frequency and degree?

If you "wake up" in the middle of a conversation, the most emotionally intelligent thing to do is tell the truth. Stop the speaker and say, "I am so sorry; my mind drifted.

Here is the last thing I remember." There may be temporary disappointment or rebuke for your mind drift, depending upon the relationship, but you will find that honesty about mind drift is the best strategy in dealing with the speaker you neglected. If the speaker wants to know what you were thinking about, you may not know. Minds don't ask for permission when they drift.

What about the flip side of the drifting issue? Suppose you are talking and someone you are speaking to gazes off into the distance or otherwise disengages. This one is easy. Just stop talking. Wait. Both as a listener and a talker you need to pay attention to the body language of those you are with. It's worth stressing again that more half of communication is body language. This is especially true when tone and body language diverge. One of the most important body parts with respect to paying attention involves the eyes because we are trained early on as children to "Look at me when I am talking to you." It is one of those things that parents say. But as you have learned in this book, you need to get the big picture as well.

But when it comes to paying attention, the eyes are a key. You can train yourself to tell whether someone has drifted away from you. As you move and take in a speaker, glance at his or her eyes. If the person's eyes look off into the distance, the individual is drifting. When the person's eyes look away, just stop talking. The person will likely look back at you and then you can start talking again. Try it.

Besides the eyes, as you take in the entire person, you can notice body language like fidgeting. As you get very advanced in observing everyone about someone's communication, you will begin to notice whether they show tension. Are their shoulders up or down? How is their breathing? Reading people is work and will test and train your powers of observation.

Mind drift is a real detriment to listening and you need to become aware of your failure to stick with the communication.

In a group setting, your newly acquired skill of getting the big picture will help you because you are now observing how others are taking in information. Is everyone drifting with this speaker? Individuals in groups start to mimic one another's reactions. I am sure you are familiar with the term "breaking the ice." This phrase refers to boats that would break the ice so they could explore the polar regions; it also relates to methods used in socially awkward situations. Well, many meetings in business are "socially awkward." Notice what happens when someone is speaking and the group—you can feel it from their body language—disagrees. Finally, someone may speak up and "break the ice." Now others will jump in. Group dynamics are fascinating and very observable if you are getting the big picture.

One of the most embarrassing interpersonal situations is to be caught ignoring someone who is earnestly trying to convey something to you. Our active minds drift. You can reduce the likelihood of mind drift by staying physically engaged, focused, and tension-free, and engaging with the speaker physically. A great conversation is like a dance—rhythmic and fun. Remember the importance of body language and tone.

EXERCISE

1. **Every time you exchange with someone, pay attention to the speaker's face and body language.** If your eyes move, your mind wanders. Keep actively engaged with the speaker. There are an infinite number of things to observe while you are listening to someone. Constantly find new things that are interesting about the speaker's tone, rhythm, gestures, and body language. Tie your observations in with the speech and content. Think about it. If you want to change your mind, you change your gaze. By keeping your eyes focused, your mind is more likely to stay focused. Embrace the tone of the speaker. Enjoy the tone and tempo of speech of the person with whom you are

engaged. This will help you focus. Enjoy their differences.

2. **Avoiding distractions.** Pocket your PDA or other device. There are countless modern distractions from tweets, texts, email, ringing phones, and so forth. Nowadays, if you can see or even feel your device, it triggers you to check it. Try to hold your PDA in your hand for one hour without checking to see who is "pinging" you one way or another. Set the timer on the clock of your PDA and work to extend your ability to ignore it longer and longer. This is a difficult exercise!

3. **Make a daily list of what is on your mind.** Certainly before a major conversation, meeting, sales call, or interview, breathe and be aware of your tension. What is bothering you? What is on your mind? Write it down on paper if you use that or on your notes app if you use one. Clear your mind. If you come into a conversation with tension, even unrelated to the speaker, you will not get much out of the conversation. These tensions are often the result of another matter you're thinking about so it is important to "shelve" those things somewhere in your mind for when you can think about them later.

4. **Don't zombie-listen.** While you should empty yourself of tension and your own thoughts in order to focus on those speaking to you, don't freeze or act unnatural. Engage with your speaker and let your body language flow with the conversation. Nod to reinforce things you agree with and withhold where you disagree. To listen well you should not interrupt, but instead influence with your body language.

5. **As you listen to someone speak, especially to someone who may, frankly, be boring, create stories around points that they make or things they say.** Storytelling exercises keep you engaged. The stranger you make the stories, the more you will remember what the speaker said and the points they made. The more interesting the stories, the more likely you are to stick with an otherwise boring talk. Study people you are going to meet with in advance. Look at pictures of them. Read about them. This will help make their content more interesting and meaningful because you can place it in context.

SUGGESTED DIALOGUE

The next time someone interrupts you, stop talking and let the person finish. When he or she is done, simply say, "Are you done with your thought?" If the person says, "No," let the person finish. If the individual says, "Yes," then simply say, "Great, I didn't want to interrupt you." This may seem passive aggressive to you, but it is the best response. Consider the alternative, "Hey, you interrupted me." This can lead to an argument over whether you were done or not. Better to make the point subtly.

CHAPTER 8

RESOLUTION- PRE- AND POST- LISTENING RITUALS

MOST PEOPLE HAVE a habit of taking conversations for granted. Whether it is a casual conversation, a meeting, or an interview, your instincts or years of interacting cause you to mostly "wing it." Speaking and listening are seen as basic life activities and therefore, we don't think we need to prepare. After all, when is the last time you thought about the stairs before you walked down a flight of stairs? That is the way we tend to view daily conversations whether they occur in the office or in a social setting.

However, you know that advance preparation and thinking will help you improve at everything you do, including breathing and walking. When you enter a martial arts class there is a routine. Punching, blocking, kicking, moving, and breathing are all natural skills also. But all martial arts classes begin with preparatory work. All classes begin with a ritual. In most, you first pay homage to the dojo, the physical structure where you will train. You take off your shoes. You change into a uniform in many martial arts. You bow as you enter and bow as you leave. You show respect for the teachers by bowing to them. You show respect for your training partners. You address instructors as Sir, Master, Sensei, or Sifu and you mean it. You warm up and you stretch. All of these rituals show a respect for the martial arts and your opponent, and prepare you for what you are about to do.

A vivid example of the attention given to human exchanges can be found in Japan. When you conduct business in Japan, there is respect with every exchange. The Japanese bow, they hand you their business card with two hands, and they exchange gifts. They make you feel special. They treat you with respect. They listen carefully, and you can feel them listen.

Great listeners, like those who are skilled at many tasks, do not wing it. They have pre-listening routines they have developed over time. They prepare. Great listeners research the people with whom they will spend time *before* they spend time with them. Great listeners consider the perspective of someone they will meet *before* they meet with them. Great listeners do their homework about the roles and biases of the participants of a meeting.

Other aspects to a pre-listening routine include cleansing yourself of tension. Empty your mind of distractions by making lists of what is on your mind. To prepare yourself for Samurai listening is work. Use the exercises in this book to develop pre-listening routines.

And in the martial arts, there are rituals after the lessons. For example, in Systema, after an hour or so of training, all of the students sit in a circle. Starting at one end of the circle, the participants talk about what they liked and how the training went. What were the best takeaways? Each person spends time usually first thanking their training partners and then discussing something he learned. This practice has several benefits. First, it prompts you to reflect on what you just did. Second, it helps you to remember what you just did. Third, it forces you to think about what you learned, what you will do differently the next time, and what you will teach someone else. Fourth, it expresses respect and appreciation for your training partners. Fifth, it is a bonding experience.

When is the last time you had a human exchange and thought ahead of time about what was going to happen? When did you last think about showing respect for the person with whom you were going to have an exchange? When is the last time after such an exchange you reflected on it in a meaningful way? When is the last time after such an exchange you thought about what you learned? What would you do differently next time? What can you now teach someone else? Did you leave the person in such a way as to thank them for their time? Did you leave them with a feeling of respect? Did you spend some time just getting closer with that person?

If you debrief at the end of every human exchange you will become a Samurai Listener very quickly. Practicing an activity means nothing if you don't receive or give yourself feedback. This resolution time—the time after an exchange—is invaluable in building your skills and in becoming a better person. It's also important to develop a pre-listening routine, which will be easy if you follow these exercises.

EXERCISE

1. **Pre-listening planning. Before your next meeting, conversation, or sales call, think about the people involved.** Do your research about their backgrounds and personal lives. When are their birthdays? What is going on in their lives? Think about what they appreciate. How can you show them your appreciation and respect? Think about pre-listening rituals.
2. **After exchange action. As you finish the exchange, express your thankfulness and**

respect. Finish the exchange by reviewing key points or takeaways. Imagine yourself in the martial arts circle. What did you appreciate about the exchange? What did you learn? What could you now teach someone else?

SUGGESTED DIALOGUE

Before beginning a meeting, if you are leading it, develop a pre-meeting ritual. This should include the following statements. "Thank you all for coming, I know you have a lot of other things to do. We will work to make this a valuable use of your time. Before we get started, you have seen the agenda I shared, is there anything you would like to cover that I have missed? I would also be interested in understanding your goals for this meeting." If no one responds, go around the room and force dialogue in case you are dealing with some introverts.

After the meeting, review the agenda and the list of "to-dos." Do not end the meeting until you have "sign off" from everyone. Free yourself and those around you from wasteful, perfunctory conversations and meetings. By doing so, you will likely find that your team will be getting more done and working well together.

CHAPTER 9

EMOTIONS— WHO IS IN CONTROL? ARE YOU?

HAVE YOU EVER watched a bout between two combatants? It could have been a boxing match, an MMA contest like UFC, a wrestling contest, or another physical contest. It could also have been a debate. There were certainly many debates between Republicans seeking the nomination for president in the year leading up to the 2016 election. Did you observe that out-of-control folks often get "knocked out" and the "cooler cats" tend to win? Did you notice at how effective Donald Trump was to destabilize his debate opponents? Did you watch how he used the emotions of his adversaries to keep them off balance?

Whether you are speaking or listening, the ability to control both your emotions and monitor and manage those who are in conversations or meetings with you is a powerful communicating tool. As an example, consider how Trump gave all his adversaries a pejorative nickname. Ted Cruz was "Lying Ted." Hillary Clinton was "Crooked Hillary." These veteran politicians with years of experienced were immediately put on the defensive by Trump's use of this provocative technique. It was a common "weapon" in his debates.

The presence of weapons evokes emotions like fear. And fear, as we saw in the presidential election, inhibits performance. In the martial arts generally we study and practice how to handle weapons when we have none. We practice being unarmed and facing someone with a knife, for example. Many martial arts arose within repressed populations who were forbidden the ownership of weapons, and so they had to defend themselves, often against government oppression, with their bare hands. The word "Karate" literally means "empty hand." How we train to not get emotional when a weapon is introduced would have been helpful to the people who were on the receiving end of the weapon of provocative speech Trump employed.

In the Russian Martial Arts called Systema, we are taught to breathe and move naturally exercising our natural instincts in response to weapons. At a recent knife seminar, the only emotion my teacher, Vladmir

Vasiliev, seemed to have was pure joy judging from his movement and the look on his face. My teacher was like a child playing with a toy. There was no anxiety. There was no fear. There was simply soft and fluid movement. His movements were natural. On the other hand, emotional responders flail around or use hard and rigid techniques; they are easy prey.

The same is true in our speech and listening. What happens when speakers and listeners are full of emotion? They tend to lose it. They tend to stop breathing properly. They tend to speak without thinking. They tend to stop listening. Whatever we have been taught about good listening and good speaking, these techniques disappear and are overridden by our anger. Emotions make us worse, not better, when it comes to human exchange.

Handling someone under emotional stress is something that takes understanding and practice. There is a right way of handling someone under stress. Doing it incorrectly makes matters worse, not better. You can test this theory yourself; the next time you are in a heated discussion, conversation, or argument, tell the other person to "calm down." You will not get that reaction. The person will not "calm down." In fact, he is likely to ratchet it up, just the opposite of what you suggest. Or perhaps you might get in return, "*You* calm down." Or, you might get, "Don't tell *me* what to do." With strong emotions, the gloves come off and the ears close. We move inward and mentally circle our wagons.

Recently, I was training with one of my long-term friends. We earned our black belts in Karate together. We were sparring with each other, and I inadvertently was more aggressive than I should have been with a particular blow. He immediately dropped his disciplined training and started flailing at me like an untrained person. He said, "Hey, were you trying to hurt me or what?" I just moved out of his way as his movements became ineffective and frantic. Of course, I apologized for my earlier aggressive move and we both laughed about it, but his emotional response was real and turned him into an undisciplined novice. That ruined the opportunity for either of us to learn from each other.

Some people find it hard to take blame but, in fact, taking the blame can be the best diffusing technique imaginable for heated exchanges. When I was at the Union Pacific Railroad managing the airfreight company, we had an unfortunate incident with one of the railroad's major clients, at the time named Grumman Aircraft. We were shipping a piece for a plane via special delivery for the manufacturer's assembly line in Bethpage, New York. It was a critical shipment. I don't remember whose fault it was, but somewhere along the line, the piece was delayed. The result was that an assembly line that built the aircraft was shut down. The company was a major customer of the railroad so my superiors were very nervous about this service failure.

Grumman wanted somebody's hide. I traveled to New York from St. Louis and let the executives scream, vent, or whatever they wanted to do. I received my "invitation" from the head of the affected Grumman division. There were lots of Grumman staff copied on the memorandum/invitation that was faxed to me and others at the railroad. I did my best to research the players in the room (this is pre-Google and pre-internet, so researching people was much harder). The head of the Grumman division that had been affected had been a World War II flying ace. I was dreading the meeting. I knew I was going to get a whupping.

When I arrived at the facility, I was directed to a large boardroom. As I took a seat, I noticed pictures on the wall of the flying ace's plane and all the planes he had downed. In a moment, it struck me that there was no way to defend what had happened. I simply had to take the blame. Eight Grumman people filed into the room; four sat on each side. I was sitting on the end. Finally, in walked the WWII ace. I had figured out that he was going to teach his staff how to dress down a vendor, and I was right.

Before he could begin, I spoke and fell on my sword. I took the blame before he could give it. I accepted the responsibility before he could bestow it. I told him he deserved a better supplier than us. I said everything I could imagine him saying. He said, "Actually you have been a good supplier and I think this is the first issue we have had with you." We then had a non-emotional constructive conversation about service. Upon my return to the railroad, I was a hero because the feedback was that good. When in doubt, set your ego aside and be aggressive about taking the blame.

To manage your own emotions, you need to practice breathing and practice putting yourself in the situations you will be in when you perform. For example, if speaking in front of others makes you nervous, force yourself to do it. If speaking in meetings makes you nervous, find things to say and come prepared to do so. Only by doing something like this over and over again will you get to a comfort level where you can lose your emotions.

To manage the emotions of others you need to consider them in your pre-listening routine. What makes them happy and unhappy? Begin conversations with disarming compliments and begin meetings with icebreakers. Avoid topics that will set them off and close their mind, or certainly don't begin with them without realizing their impact on the other's behavior. Use your observational skills to read the body language and nonverbal cues to monitor when you are heading into "dangerous" emotional territory.

EXERCISE

1. **Before you meet with someone, spend some time thinking about what might embarrass, ignite, or set the individual off course.** Avoid those topics and mannerisms that will derail the person with whom you are interacting. Some people tend to the defensive. The better you know a person, the more likely you will know what sets them off and what drives them from the rational to the emotional realm. To calm others, you need to know these aspects of their personality. In long-term relationships, you know how to push some buttons instead of others that will cause someone to get upset.

2. **Be assertive and take the blame, even if it is only partially your fault.** It is easy and will soften your exchanges. In your coming conversations, practice saying, "I'm sorry." Practice saying, "It was my fault."

3. **Practice forgetting about yourself.** Focus on the other person and use the breathing exercises in this book.

107

SUGGESTED DIALOGUE

Practice diffusing emotions in conversations. Suppose that you have an employee from whom you need something or suppose the employee has just been asked to perform an assignment. If he feels he is overworked, then the pushback may well come in the form of emotional conversation. My suggested advice is to let the individual vent and do not disagree or argue in any respect. "I can't believe that Bob thinks I have time to run those calculations. I am two weeks late already on a project for Sally. Who do they think I am? They aren't paying me enough for this level of work!" Options? You could say simply confirm the fact and say, "Yes, I agree, they are being unreasonable." But how much help is that? Instead, I suggest you help get the employee talking more in a way that helps him solve the problem. How about saying, "I hate it when I get conflicting assignments with crazy expectations; it happens to me too. I tend to ask myself who do I mind disappointing more, because someone is going to be disappointed." The aggrieved person needs to make a choice. Help him think about and make the choice he has to make. Or you can say, "Well, maybe you should have Sally and Bob work it out. I have done that before." Go a step beyond diffusing emotions and help the person walk towards a practical solution.

CHAPTER 10

SENSES–THE ROLE OF OTHER SENSES AND "SENSING"

WE ALL HAVE human instincts that are sitting in limbo because the office and home environment does not bring them out in us. And yet these instincts can be extremely helpful in those environments. So the question is, given that the instincts can't be trained in the office environments, how can we get in touch with them to use them in those environments? This is an example of bringing playground or physical education skills to bear in a classroom (now office) environment.

Every other year, those who practice Systema are invited to an outdoor camp for training for a week in the Algonquin forest in northern Canada. During training there is a drill that helps practitioners get back in touch with their instincts and train themselves to heighten their sense of awareness of another. These exercises are done repeatedly in the daylight, at dusk, and in the dark.

The drill starts with just two people. One person (the aggressor) stands about 30 meters from the other (the passive person). The aggressor forms an intention before he or she starts walking towards the passive person. The aggressor's intention is to do either harm or good will towards the passive party. The aggressor walking towards the passive person has a training knife, metal but dull. As the aggressor walks towards the passive person, he or she does not change their intent. The passive person is standing and waiting for the aggressor as the aggressor walks towards him or her. The passive person is attempting to discern the intent of the aggressor.

Does the person walking toward you mean you ill will or not? If you believe the person means you ill will, just as they reach you, you prepare to defend yourself. If you perceive the person does not mean you ill will, you do nothing. The aggressor discloses his or her intent by attacking you with the knife or by putting his hand on your shoulder very gently. The object of the exercise is to train you to ascertain the will of someone approaching you. It is training in "sensing" another. It is training to put you back in touch with instincts you have, which are latent.

The drill can also be done with three people; one passive person stands still and two aggressors walk towards the passive person from about 30 meters away. One of the two aggressors walking towards you has a knife and forms an intention of hurting you. The other is a friend and forms that intention. It is your task to figure out who is who. I have done both of these exercises for years and witnessed as everyone got better at this. It teaches you to read someone using skills you have that you don't use very often and so they atrophy. They need to be exercised to work for you.

These same intentions are present in every exchange, even verbal ones, with or without a knife. It is possible that some people naturally read these things without training because of a prior need to do so or perhaps they have trained their instincts based upon experiences. But no matter where you are on the spectrum of the skill of sensing, you can improve with practice and training. And this ability can be a key differentiator in your ability to succeed.

The key to sensing others is to lose yourself. This will take some explaining. Our ability to feel others means we have to lose our own tension and get beyond ourselves. I can't feel you if all I feel is me. Have you ever had a hurt hip or knee? Perhaps you have experienced arthritis or had an injury? Where is your focus? What is on your mind? What obsesses your mind? You keep coming back to the knee or hip. It draws you in and consumes you. What do you or can you feel about someone else? Nothing. In fact, you become unaware of any other sensations in your body.

Have you ever had a particle of food stuck in your teeth and you can't get it out? What do you do? You obsess over it. You work your tongue to dislodge it. You brush your teeth. You find a toothpick. But it consumes you and your mind keeps coming back to it. You are not in a position to "feel" how someone else is reacting to you.

When one trains with martial arts champions, they can feel you. They can sense you. They know what you will do next. How do they know? While their experience matters, their sensing skills come from being free of their own pain and tension. They empty themselves and therefore they know that what they are feeling is coming from you, not them. When you're in pain or under stress you will not have the ability to sense others.

Think about professional poker players. They are excellent at relaxing and reading others. Have you noticed some players will wear sunglasses in professional competitions? This is their way of "disappearing." This is their way of hiding themselves. For those who are less inclined to get physical and do some physical training, a poker "habit" can provide you with some of these same skills.

Many of the listening issues get in the way of our ability to sense others. If you are not aware, if you are not receptive, if you are not engaged, if you are not understanding, if you are not persistent, if you are not resolution oriented, if you are full of emotion, if you are not in touch with your senses, if you are egotistical and only focused on yourself, if you are nervous and out of pace with your conversation partner then you will not be able to sense them. In other words, sensing someone is a byproduct of incorporating all the strategies that you've been reading about in this book.

EXERCISE

1. **Adapt one of the exercises from Systema camp.** Get yourself a training partner and have the person walk towards you with an intention. Work on reading the person by getting the big picture. Take in the big picture. Now check yourself internally. Breathe and look for signs of tension. Do you have tension? Work to clean yourself through segmented tension exercises.

2. **Work to discern someone's intent from his or her body language.** There are many resources on body language. One way to do this is to reverse engineer an encounter. Suppose you have a meeting and in the meeting, someone you don't know comes at you in an aggressive way. What were the individual's behaviors

leading up to the exchange? Were there clues or signals that you can remember?

3. **Learn poker.** There is a reason for the term "poker face." Practice working to read when people are bluffing and when they have good hands.

SUGGESTED DIALOGUE

Practice checking your instincts through dialogue by verifying what someone is feeling. If someone seems unhappy, say, "Are you okay?" Try to discern his emotion. If you know he isn't okay and you are worried about his reaction, attribute the emotion to yourself. Suppose the two of you are waiting for a meeting or something else to happen. Check your sense of him by saying, "I am so tired of waiting for this meeting, aren't you?" Use yourself to diffuse the risk of being wrong.

CHAPTER 11

EGO – AVOIDING THE "ME" THAT GETS IN THE WAY

WE ALL LIKE ourselves, right? We wake up in the morning and look in the mirror and we say, "Hey, you are the coolest cat I know." After all, it is only ourselves that lives in our body. A healthy amount of this is good-quality self-esteem. There is a spectrum of self-esteem from the extreme of "I am the only person that matters and exists," to the other end, which is "Everyone matters but me." Self-esteem appears to be one of those traits around which statistics experts would say there is a normal distribution, meaning that the bulk of people have a healthy amount of self-esteem with much smaller but equal numbers of egotists and low self-esteem folks at the extremes. And some people may have self-esteem sometimes but not others, and they may have self-esteem about some things but not others. Too much self-esteem can hurt your ability to communicate, and too little can hurt it as well.

Egotistical folks, those who have too much self-esteem, can be bad listeners because they don't respect the opinion of others. The love of self is often inconsistent with respect for others and their opinions. People who love themselves tend to have all the answers, which means they're probably going to close themselves off to further learning. In a sense, they are right. They *do* know it all. They have all the answers that they will ever have.

There is a high correlation between egotistical people and people who dominate conversations. A high love for oneself means a high love for that self's opinions. If you examine ARE U PRESENT you can see how ego inhibits every necessary skill for human exchange. If you have high ego, you are less aware of others. If you have high ego, you are less receptive to others. If you have high ego, you will not engage in fair, balanced, and bargained-for exchanges. If you have high ego, you will not put yourself in someone else's shoes. Perspective listening will be a non-starter. Your only attempt at understanding will be to get someone else to understand you.

Martial arts emphasize humility and loss of ego. That is why these activities are so good for kids. They teach compassion and mercy that come from being strong and knowing how to defend yourself. "The stronger you are, the more merciful you can be," is a common theme in a dojo.

A great contrast to this attitude is found in the movie *The Karate Kid*. At the Cobra Kai Dojo (the bad guys) the instructor says, "We do not train to be merciful here. The enemy deserves no mercy." It is made very clear and obvious to all of us that this is not the way. In large part this movie is about good and evil and the traits of those in one camp or the other. Mr. Miyagi is a humble, unassuming man with no ego. Mr. Cleese (the "evil" teacher) is an egomaniac. The Karate contests are about him winning. He is anxious to show off his skills. Mr. Miyagi only uses Karate as a last resort for defense.

The motto of Systema is "Strength, Courage and Humility." Humility is heavily emphasized. Humility begets learning. The vessel needs to be empty in order to take in information and the soul needs to be humble.

But being too low on self-esteem is not good for communication either. And this is where you need to be sensitive to introverts. Introverts may be shy and have low self-esteem and worry that they have nothing useful to say. But research does not show them to be less intelligent; in fact, quite the opposite could be true according to some studies.

It is your duty as an extrovert, it is your duty as a leader, to help these people express themselves. They have opinions; they have valid opinions. They just don't value them, but you should.

EXERCISE

1. **Soften your ego.** We tend increasingly as we get older and can control who is around us, to surround ourselves with people who positively reinforce us. As humans, we seek pleasure over pain. These folks tend to reinforce our ego. Here are several strategies to dull that tendency. Put yourself in an environment where you are forced to interact with strangers. Do you remember summer camp when you were young? Some kids liked you and some kids didn't. You had to deal with that. Often you had to adjust your own behavior in order to get along and build community.

2. **Seek feedback.** If you are a manager, get reviews from your people. Getting honest and direct feedback can be humbling but it will improve your leadership and communication skills tremendously.

SUGGESTED DIALOGUE

If you are heavy on the ego front and closer to the end of the spectrum where egotism lies, work to communicate with less "ego" by reducing your use of the pronouns "me" or "I" or "my" or "mine." It is something I am actively working to do, and it helps according to those with whom I communicate. Instead of saying, "I want this and I want it now," say, "It would be helpful if we had this now."

If you are an introvert, practice speaking up; the world needs to hear your opinions. And those of us who work around introverts need to be constantly saying to them, "What do you think?"

Master the art of listening to introverts. Practice conversing with quiet and shy individuals. Work to engage them and learn what makes them excited to speak. They don't speak much so when they do, it will tell you a lot.

CHAPTER 12

NERVES– THE IMPACT OF TENSION

Breathing and Listening

THE FIRST THING we do when we are born is breathe. If we don't, we get a slap so we are forced to breathe. The last thing we do before we die is take our last breath. And who helps us learn to breathe between our first and last breath? No one. It is considered an auto response. It is considered programmatic. Unless you are a professional athlete, the only encounters you may have with breathing lessons are when you practice yoga, meditation, and martial arts. As a result, most people don't realize the power of breathing patterns and the power that can come from working with your breathing.

In Karate, you learn to discharge a powerful breath as you complete a move. This is part of the purpose of the Kiai that you hear Karate practitioners make when they are completing a strike. It is the yell Karate practitioners perform as they complete a move. The problem with this breathing technique is it causes you to hold your breath. When your breath stops, your movement stops, your mind stops, and then everything comes to a halt.

Proper breathing brings proper movement, relaxation, and readiness. Controlling your breathing also helps you control your inner self, which affects the vibe (or aura, call it what you will) that you give off to other participants in a conversation, and it affects your ability to absorb and remember information through speech or other senses.

While all martial arts emphasize some aspect of breathing study and training, Systema, The Russian Martial Arts has the most comprehensive set of breathing principles. Here are a few key principles you learn from studying and practicing Systema:

Become conscious of your breathing. Be aware of your breathing. Check yourself. When we are tense, we take short breaths. When we are relaxed, we take longer breaths. So, if you want to be relaxed, slow your breathing. If you want to energize yourself, breathe short breaths.

Breathe in through your nose and out through your mouth.

Feel your body react to your breathing and what muscles are engaged.

As you do exercises or any daily activities, be conscious of your in-and-out breathing. If you swing a golf club, for example, try breathing in on the back swing and breathing out on the swing.

Be conscious not to hold your breath.

Breathe continuously. Don't stop breathing.

Make your breathing natural; don't take in any more air than you need.

Use breathing and walking exercises. As you take a step, breathe in and then take another step and breathe out. You can extend these to two steps breathing in, and two steps breathing out, and mix them up. Try to inhale on one step and exhale on two. Find patterns that make you feel better. At different times, different strategies will feel different to you. You can build up your energy with fewer steps and calm yourself with long breaths associated with multiple steps.

(For more on these techniques, read *Secrets of the Russian Breath Masters* by Vladimir Vasiliev.)

You will be a better listener if you can control your breathing and breath patterns. As you become conscious of your own patterns, guess what happens? You will become conscious of the breath patterns of others, thereby allowing you to understand where they are coming from in a much deeper way. Become aware of yourself and you will "disappear."

To understand the concept of disappearing requires some extra explanation. Imagine you are trying to hear a sound. As you strain to make it out, you try to isolate it. Your method for isolating that sound will be to identify other sounds and exclude them or turn them into background noise or eliminate them if you can. Suppose you are camping and you hear a noise outside your tent. What is the first thing that you do? You ask everyone to hush. You are asking them to "disappear" so you can sense the sound.

Consequently, the act of "disappearing" involves you identifying the "noise" inside of you. Relaxing and eliminating that noise and tension allows you to feel others and isolate to their sound and rhythm. Once you "disappear," the people around you will seem larger than life and their actions and words will appear louder than you can imagine. You will "hear" everyone.

Some environments are better than others for you to begin this practice. You need an environment where you can get away and clear your mind if you want to be a better listener. Going into the woods, sitting by the ocean or taking in a lake are great opportunities to practice isolating sounds. These are places where you can get back in touch with your instincts. Vacations to these places can help you practice listening techniques because you should be more relaxed and in a better position to "disappear."

EXERCISE

1. **Practice the breathing and walking exercises described above every day.**

2. **Eliminate the practice of multitasking.** This does a disservice to both the person whose email you are reading and the person at your door. Explain to whoever is at your "open door" that you need a minute to finish what you are doing.

3. **Control your self-talk.** Pay attention to what you say to yourself and make it more positive over time.

4. **Control your breathing.** Become aware and train your breathing so you can improve your ability to take in information.

5. **Disappear.** Get to know yourself so deeply that you can erase yourself and only feel and hear the other.

SUGGESTED DIALOGUE

Each day when you wake in the morning say to yourself, "I am going to be a better listener today and work to learn from those around me by increasing my openness to the views of others."

CHAPTER 13

TEMPO–GETTING IN TOUCH WITH RHYTHM

WE SPEND A lot of time teaching content in sales and negotiation settings. One of the hardest things to understand is the intangible element known as instinct, timing, or charisma. It is what in the end differentiates the closers and the people who get deals done on their terms. It is the part of sales and negotiation that engineers and technical people sometimes find hard to understand. Some think it cannot be taught. But it is teachable. Great negotiators have strong technical skills and training, but what they also do well is listen carefully and get in touch with the rhythm of the person or people on the other side. They are in touch with the back-and-forth; like great Samurai in combat, they are Samurai in human exchanges.

To understand and feel rhythm takes practice. There are many ways to understand the rhythm of human exchange. The best way for you to understand and learn to feel rhythm will be based on what hobbies you practice. Do you like to listen to music? Do you enjoy dancing? Do you like to travel to different areas of the world or your country? Each of these can provide you with some broad arrays of human exchange from a tempo perspective.

Martial arts range from the rapid-fire movements of Karate to the slow rhythms of Tai Chi. It is not unusual for youthful practitioners to learn and spend time on arts like Tae Kwan Do and kickboxing and, as they age, to move to deeper more internal arts with slower movements and tempos but with each move executed with deeper meaning and sensing.

Do you have a sense of your own rhythm when it comes to human exchange? Are you a fast talker or a slow talker? Where are you from? What are the speech patterns of people from your part of the world? If you travel you can tell the difference between the pace of human exchange in New York versus Texas. Someone from Chicago exchanges with other humans very differently than someone from New Orleans. And it is not just North and South. Urban speech patterns and rural speech patterns differ greatly. Gender and ethnic differences can lead to different speech patterns as well.

I personally enjoy watching my friend from Midland, Texas, an oil-rich town in west Texas, interact with my friend from Manchester, England, because like any other concept, to understand rhythm in people it is best to start with extremes. My friend from Midland, like others from the more rural South or Southwest, tends to turn single syllable words into two or three words. If you are from the North or from an urban area you will simply say the word "feet" to describe where your legs meet the ground. My Midland friend says something that sounds more like "fee-at" and it takes him twice as long to say it.

If you don't get to travel, then you can use movies or TV shows to help you gain an understanding of these differences or watch politicians or commentators from different parts of the world. Perhaps you watched the political debates for the recent presidential election cycle. Contrast the rapid fire of Ted Cruz and Marco Rubio, both from Cuba, with the slow and deliberate style of Ben Carson at the Republican debates. On the Democratic side of the aisle contrast the fast-talking Elizabeth Warren from Boston with Bernie Saunders from the more rural Vermont. These speech patterns matter in human exchange and your ability to communicate well with others in a personal or business context depends in part on your ability to read and adapt to these varying styles.

As a result of my writing I have appeared on a lot of radio and TV shows, and I have enjoyed them. Often, but not always, I am not in the same room with the interviewer. I am on the phone as I am being interviewed. I try to research the host of the show as much as I can. While I do not have the luxury of all the other indications like body language, facial expressions, and other cues that would be extremely helpful in communicating, I do have the ability to sense and respond to their tempo.

I recall an early morning drive-time radio show with a male host from a city in the Northeast talking about my first book, *STAGNation*, which was about the recession in the jobs economy. You don't immediately talk with the host. A producer comes on the phone and explains whom you will speak with and then tells you he will connect you. In the meantime, you can hear the host. This particular host spoke fast, really fast. It was like a machine gun. I knew that in order to communicate effectively with him, I was going to have to move fast. Once I was talking with the host and he said in rapid fire fashion, "Cash, are we in a STAGNation?" I came right back to him at a pace matching his, "Yes, Bruce, I believe we are and here is why..." He loved it. I got feedback after the interview that he thought it was one of his best shows. That's because I matched his rhythm.

In contrast, later that afternoon, I was on another show that was definitely touchy feely. I listened to the host as I was waiting to be introduced. She was caring, warm, thoughtful, and deep. I immediately adapted to that style. "Cash, a lot of my friends are having trouble finding work; why?" My response was caring and warm. "Frankie, I am sorry to hear that and I am hearing this all too often, there aren't enough good jobs to go around and the jobs that do exist are somewhere else and require some other skill." It couldn't have been more different than the morning interview. I have to say, both exchanges were excellent from my perspective and from what I heard from the audience's perspective. Rhythm matters a lot to people. It is part of the give and take we discussed when talking about fair exchanges.

If you are into dance, contrast ballet to square dancing and to modern dance. If you are into music listen to the blues then hip-hop then rock and roll. There are underlying rhythms and tempos. Face-to-face sales or negotiation is a like a dance, a song, a rhythmic exchange. Points and counterpoints are exchanges of words and also emotion. There is a rhythm to human exchanges. If you want to test what I am talking about, try some of the following exercises.

To listen effectively in a conversation, you can't just listen to the words and you can't just watch the body language and intonation. You need to listen for, feel, and get in sync with the rhythm. Are you in a waltz? A techno-dance? A tango? Find some art you really understand that has different rhythms. Everyone you sit across from has a natural rhythm they have developed. Gain an advantage by figuring out what it is.

As a martial artist, I use slow rhythms like Tai Chi and fast rhythms like Karate to describe in my mind the virtual human movement I am feeling in sales or negotiating. For my own personal style, I really love using a Jiu Jitsu rhythm for sales because it is a gentle martial art that involves thinking about what someone is going to do next, and feeling the person before he or she moves. It has a wonderful flow to it. Maybe you love music. Use the different music rhythms to keep you in touch.

Silence, which we explore in the next chapter, is truly golden when it comes to rhythm. What is my best tip for handling silence if you are trying to sell or trying to get a point in negotiation? Be quiet yourself. Respond in kind. In our noisy world today, we have lost the gift of silence. Those who practice silence are like modern Jedi knights, practicing a long-lost martial art. Practitioners of many martial arts spend lots of time being quiet and relaxing so they can feel others, not themselves.

There is one sure-fire way to lose touch with the rhythm of a human exchange, and that is to bring stress to the situation. If you enter an exchange with stress, you will never feel the rhythm of the other people. All you will feel is yourself.

Winners respect rhythm and know how to sense it and change it up. Pay attention to the rhythm of your exchanges with other humans, and learn how to use rhythm to redirect and win sales and negotiations.

EXERCISE

1. **Have a conversation with a friend or significant other.** Say something you know the person will disagree with. What do you get? The individual will likely argue with you, picking up the pace in the process. Saying something controversial tends to turn up the heat and get things moving faster. Want to slow things down? Say something obvious or repetitive. Try this. In general, you can change the tempo of a face-to-face exchange simply by deciding whether to say something controversial or something obvious. You can affect tempo by agreeing or disagreeing with your counterpart.

2. **Specifically, in a sales or negotiation context, if you are not making progress and getting lots of objections, you are not going to advance your sale by arguing.** You need to back off and slow down. Say something obvious that no one can disagree with to regain your footing. You need to get them "nodding" in agreement with you and regain your footing. Notice that this is consistent with the technical side

of need-satisfaction sales. If you are having trouble closing, remind your prospects of the benefits they have already accepted.

3. **Work to understand your own personal rhythm.** Who do you think you are like from the perspective of speech patterns? Find a commentator, politician or actor that you think has your speech pattern. Watch this professional adapt their speech pattern to their situation. Watch them use their own rhythm to their advantage. Watch them use silence as part of their rhythm.

SUGGESTED DIALOGUE

In an interview, someone says, "Where do you see your-self in five years?" Your response should be designed around their pace. If she has have exhibited a rapid pace, she is likely expecting a "Red Bull" type response. So both in tempo and substance, you should be aggres-sive in your goals. Perhaps you can say something like, "At a fast-paced company like ABC, I expect I will be pre-sented with continual challenges where I can contribute and grow and take on increasingly responsible roles which will allow me to further strengthen and build this dynamic company."

If, on the other hand the pace of the person and envi-ronment is slower and thoughtful, your response might be, "I look forward to gaining increasing responsibility and being a good team member and contributor as I learn more about the business and the industry and the people."

CHAPTER 14

SILENCE-THE MOST POWERFUL COMMUNICATION DEVICE

Embracing the Power of Silence

CHANCES ARE YOU have been in a conversation, negotiation, a meeting, or on a sales call when there is a gap in the conversation and then someone jumps in to fill the silence. If it is a sales call, whether you're the buyer or part of a sales team including the salesperson, you will cringe. It is hard to watch. It is hard to listen to and observe. If someone is selling to you, you want to say, "Shut up and let me think." If you are in a conversation or negotiation, you have lost an opportunity to let someone absorb what was being said. Never, ever disrespect the value and power of silence in a human exchange, especially in a sales or negotiation scenario. Learn to respect the power of silence in all human exchange.

Selling is about getting people to change their behavior. Regardless of all the math and financial ROIs that go into it, changing behavior involves emotions. If it didn't, we wouldn't need sales people. But we do. Human change is a human process involving subtle cues and deeply human exchanges. We are all looking for buying signals. Do you know the ultimate buying signal from a prospect? Silence. In that moment of silence the prospect is imagining buying from you. The person is imagining what he or she will tell their existing supplier. He or she is imagining what to say to peers, the manager, or procurement.

The world seems to contain an overabundance of noise and advice. Consider the fundamental law of supply and demand. The supply and demand curves tell us that as supply goes up, if demand stays the same, price goes down. This is a fundamental law of microeconomics. And sure enough, advice these days (including the millions of blogs and LinkedIn Posts) is free. Economics is working. It is noisy out there. So if it is noisy out there, what is in short supply? Silence.

People pay for meditation, yoga, and trips to the woods or mountains—anyplace to get away from the noise. If you live in a city, you know how noisy it can be between sirens, motorcycles, construction, dogs barking, and neighbors. And it is not just about having quiet time for sleep. Daytime silence is important as well. The workplace itself has become much noisier as well.

More and more offices are using open-seating with everyone working in cubicles or perhaps even around a table. While it's important to be accessible, not everyone can think in these settings. So many great thoughts, ideas, and inventions have come during periods of meditation or daydreaming. Whether Newton was or was not hit in the head with an apple, by contemporaneous accounts, he was actually daydreaming in the garden the day he "discovered" gravity. Silence is a cool and productive state. It is a state wherein you concentrate, think, contemplate, and invent.

Do you remember the last time you were in deep thought and a noise interrupted it? Or maybe someone interrupted you and you lost your train of thought. What did you think of that thing or person that so rudely interrupted your blessed silence? Your self-talk turned to hatred and you said, "Why can't they shut that dog up?" Or you said, "Do we really have to do the dishes right now?" Or maybe you said, "You interrupted me and now I can't remember what I was going to say." Imagine what your prospects think of you when you interrupt their thinking.

How hard is it to find a great prospect? How many emails do you have to send to get a phone contact? How many phone contacts do you have to make to get a face-to-face call? How many meetings do you need to have to get the actual decision-maker in the room? After all that work, do you decide to interrupt the silence?

Say less and listen more on sales calls. It is that simple. As your prospects or decision-makers are listening to you and pondering, when you are done, be done. Let them have their time. They are studying you and what you said. Sit back, relax, and wait. If you have the patience, you will see that buying signal. It will first be manifested in body language, not words. You may see their eyes look off into the distance; you may see them stare at your ROI model or other handout. And while they do that, be still. Be quiet. Worship the silence that is there.

Imagine a peaceful place that you love. I like to think of Lake Tahoe or the old cemetery that sits on the hillside on the road to Cortona, Italy.

EXERCISE

1. **Pay attention to the gaps in conversations in which you participate.** Notice the discomfort many seem to have with these conversation gaps. Resist the temptation to fill gaps and pauses. Take it in. Let it sit.
2. **If you are leading a meeting, structure input and structure gaps.** In group meetings,

oftentimes the lack of gaps has to do with the fact that everyone is trying to impress the leader. People are fighting for "airtime." You can structure input so that everyone knows they will get a crack at giving input. Going around the room is a good way to ensure everyone will have input. Announce at the beginning of the meeting that you will do this so people can relax.

SUGGESTED DIALOGUE

Bite your tongue during pauses. Imagine what you would have said in a meeting and wait to see if someone else says it. When they do, don't say, "I thought of that." Don't say, "I was going to say that." Let it be. Be thinking not about what you were going to say, but think through if you said "A" what are some potential responses. Then you will be ready when someone else raises your point to take it to the next level. Silence can help you think ahead and beyond where you usually do.

CHAPTER 15

LISTENING AND LEADING

BECAUSE PART OF what leaders do is give speeches, they may leave you with the impression that great leading is about talking and speaking. But if you admire what people say, consider that their words, their sincerity, their honesty, and their content is borrowed from people to whom they listened and with whom they were engaged.

Great leaders are intense listeners and have the ability to take the many things that they hear and the many people with whom they interact and turn it into action-oriented, empathetic speech.

Leaders gain respect by earning it. Leaders earn respect by respecting others. One of the best, if not the best way to show someone that you respect them, is to listen to them. Great leaders don't just "hear" others; they honor the ARE U PRESENT principles. They are aware, receptive, engaged, understanding, persistent, seek resolution and keenly aware of emotions, senses, ego, nerves, and tempo.

In 1986, the Union Pacific Railroad bought Overnite Transportation, a trucking company. Mergers between regulated transportation companies at the time required approval of the Interstate Commerce Commission. To gain approval, you had to show that the merger or acquisition was in the public interest and specifically had to show that the trucking company was going to benefit the shipping public and enhance rail operations.

A merger team was put together for the deal and began working on the process to gain ICC approval of the transaction. There was a lot at stake because the Railroad had made a tender offer for the company, and it already owned the stock in a blind trust. If it did not gain approval it would have to resell the acquired shares back in the open market. The Railroad had paid quite a premium for the shares, which it would lose upon any resale. The stakes were high enough that it was one of the primary projects of the Railroad's new CEO, Mike Walsh.

The acquisition team's first encounter with Mike was on one of the private jets the Railroad owned. We were flying from Omaha, where the Railroad was headquartered, to Richmond, Virginia, where the trucking company was headquartered. Trying to get to anywhere from Omaha was a challenge commercially or at least it would take a full day, so the team was told to report to a hanger.

What happened when we got on the plane surprised us, not because there was assigned seating based upon seniority, we expected that, but because there was a breakfast tray. And guess who served everybody? Mike Walsh. Once we got in our assigned seat and everyone else was situated, Mike asked each of us, "What would you like for breakfast?" Each person told him. He picked out your fruit for you. He buttered your bread. He put cream cheese on your bagel. He was the best breakfast server we had ever seen. And he listened so intently as you described what you wanted.

I still remember this vividly thirty-plus years later. During the entire flight he asked questions and engaged each of us. He wanted to know what we thought of the prospects and what the challenges were. I was twenty-six, and only one year out of law school, and this former U.S. Attorney was asking me what I thought and engaging with me in a real way.

How do I know this is great leadership? The effect this encounter had on me and everyone else was profound. We *wanted* to work hard for this guy. We *wanted* to do our best work for this gentleman. We *wanted* to exceed his expectations. He brought out the best in us because he showed us he cared about us. He helped us excel because we believed he needed us. Listening and engaging with us built his leadership. It was foundational and strong.

Anyone who experienced that became an advocate for him and his positions.

EXERCISE

1. **If you are a leader, start counting your words.** Try to ask and listen 80 percent of the time. Begin meetings with questions. Even after questions are asked, follow up with more questions. Become an inquisitive leader.

2. **If you are not yet a leader, act like an inquisitive leader and you will become one.** Be someone who brings out the best in others, not the person with the answers.

SUGGESTED DIALOGUE

If you supervise others, pick one of your direct reports and rotate them daily to speak one-on-one. Ask them a simple question, "What can I do for you today? How can I help you today? Is there anything you need I can help with?" And then do it.

CHAPTER 16

LISTENING AND SELLING

THE DATA ON asking and listening versus telling in successful sales calls is something I had to learn early on in my career. I was trained in IBM's professional selling system (PSS). The PSS system is based on asking questions, which were called "probes," to uncover opportunities that were "qualified" or refined through questions into needs that a certain product or service could resolve. In essence, the client has some unmet need that your product or service could fill, but you needed to go on a verbal quest to figure that out and pull it out of them.

This basic structure of needs satisfaction selling has helped me be successful at sales for more than thirty years. Asking and listening are the keys to a successful face-to-face selling encounter. But *what* you ask is extremely important.

If you go into a sales call and ask dumb or naïve questions, you are actually talking. You are messaging that you don't know what you are doing. Examples of dumb questions can be, "Tell me about ABC Corporation" or "What do you folks do here at this facility?" or "How many years have you been with ABC Company?" Mostly these are not good questions because you can find the answers very readily on the internet. Most people expect you to have done that basic homework before you arrive.

These days, particularly with the ability to prepare by getting information readily available online, there's no excuse for employees in sales positions to "wing it." If you have done your homework, your questions will be far more intelligent. It won't be, "tell me about your company." It will be, "I read that you are starting a new division that will produce product A; will your needs change as a result?" That question sends a message to whomever you're engaged that you cared enough to do your research, that you respect people's time enough to have come prepared, and that you are focused on their needs—not just their product. They will respond with, "We have been told nothing will change." Or, they may respond with, "We have heard we are going to get busy." Or they will respond with, "We don't know yet." Or they may say, "Funny you should ask, I now have responsibility for that also." No matter how they answer your query, you can engage. The question puts them into an active mode. The answer will make them receptive to an engaging follow up question. Remember to focus on their life, their challenges, their needs, and then slip in how you can help.

Too many salespeople come into a sales exchange like they are entering the Octagon or the Boxing ring. They are keen on "blowing away the competition." You may have to ultimately explain why your company versus another, but it should come out through normal and natural conversation.

EXERCISE

1. Imagine an interview scenario. Don't come to the interview with, I can't wait to tell you about me. Bring to the interview the desire to get the other person talking about what they need. Now you talk about how you can solve their problems. Ask, ask, and ask.

2. Count your words versus the words of your prospect on a sales call. Count your statements versus your questions. Sales calls that are 80% ask versus tell are more successful.

SUGGESTED DIALOGUE

Not, "I am completely qualified for this job, I did this exact set of tasks in my last position." Try instead, "I reviewed the job description, do you feel that it captures the biggest challenges of the position; what are the biggest challenges?"

CHAPTER 17

LISTENING AND NEGOTIATING

YOU CAN USE the ARE U PRESENT framework to become a better negotiator. In this chapter, we'll examine what it means to be aware, receptive, engaged, understanding, and persistent while being conscious of resolution, emotions, senses, ego, nerves, and tension.

Awareness in a negotiation context means understanding what you want and what they want and all the variables associated with the potential transaction or resolution. If you don't get the big picture, you will miss factors that may be negotiable. This is often the biggest impediment in a negotiation; one party hasn't clearly defined what it wants. It lacks clarity in its own goals. Step one is to analyze and understand what you or your organization wants. Step two, which also involves awareness, is having knowledge of what the other side wants. Until you clearly understand and are "aware" of what you want and what they want, negotiations cannot lead to success. If you do not know what you want, your odds of getting it go way down. If you don't know what the other side wants, you don't know what trade-offs can be made.

The most basic issue in negotiation is often overlooked or given inadequate consideration. The first task in any negotiation is figuring out what you want. This needs to be a thorough process and it often isn't. Odds are you are part of an organization that needs something and you have been tasked with getting it. How much time have you spent qualifying the task that you are given?

Suppose you own a company that produces promotional t-shirts and I ask you to source the t-shirts that will be printed or embroidered. You will probably try to figure out who did this last time, what did they pay for the shirts, and so on. Once armed with that information, you may play a few companies off against one another, including the "incumbent" company. What you should do is to identify the full scope of what you want/need first.

Being receptive in a negotiation context means that you accept that you may not get exactly what you want or exactly the price or terms you want, but you accept that and are willing to work through a process to see what you can get. Receptivity is about willingness to change. Negotiation involves compromise. Receptiveness means you use encouraging language and body language to show where there is openness to compromise. It also means you leave biases behind that may hinder you from doing a transaction.

To be engaged in a negotiation context means to be willing to "play the game" and to play it fairly. You are willing to exchange terms and engage in give and take. The give and take has to be fair also, or the deal won't happen. Sometimes people try to skip this step, but it rarely works. A party to a negotiation may try this in a couple ways. They might say, for example, "Let's forgo the back and forth here is our reasonable number." This will not likely be successful and the other party will counter it anyway. Why? Negotiation is always about engaging in the back and forth. The back and forth is a human need. Another example is with best and final offers. Near the end of a negotiation, a party may say, "Okay, this is our best and final." But in my experience there is always more negotiation after this. Engaging and fair exchange is the heart of negotiation.

Knowing that engagement is such a key part of negotiation, and that no matter what you say it is going to happen, your best bet is to think ahead about where you want to end up and imagine the back and forth that will get you there. That is what great negotiators do.

Understanding in the negotiation context means you are willing to truly see things from their perspective and you constantly work to confirm you are on the right track. This is another often overlooked and key element of negotiation. Like being receptive, perspective listening is key to perspective negotiating. Being able to get what you want means understanding what they want and why. What challenges is the other side facing? As with any good listening, listening in the context of a negotiation involves confirming progress and lack of progress on an ongoing basis.

Persistence in the negotiation context means you are willing to see it through, reduce the use of games and stick with the issues as long as it takes. Breakthroughs in negotiation often happen just as people are getting "deal fatigue."

Resolution means that you will reach agreement or recognize that no deal is going to happen. But it also means painstakingly working through each aspect and deal point. Good negotiators break down their overall objective into smaller ones. The ability to achieve a milestone in a negotiation often means gaining agreement on some basic facts. Negotiation is process. The exercises at the end of the chapter walk through an example of process-driven negotiation.

Every human exchange has some element of emotion to it, not matter how large the transaction. Often in negotiations, participants will be judged heavily by the result. Good negotiations lead to positive reviews and bonuses. For staff people in organizations, negotiations lead to concrete and measurable outcomes. It is a chance for an employee to "show his value." It is a chance for staff to show their value to an organization in hard dollar terms. "I saved us $200k on that deal." When our personal livelihood and reputations are on the line, the emotions can surface. As a result, you can use your skills managing your own and others' emotions in the negotiation context to help you succeed.

Observe body language and sense feelings to ascertain what is important to the other side and where give may occur. If you have watched some of the coverage of President Trump's international visits and dealings, you may have seen and listened to commentary from experts who specialize in body language. Watch how people shake your hand; aggressive types have aggressive handshakes. They are going to come at you hard. Open palms indicate a willingness to negotiate. These are generally not rocket science. People who look open and have open stances and gestures generally are open. Negotiations are full of nonverbal cues. You are in a position both to observe these and use these cues.

Ego means you are willing to separate the people from the problem and not just focus on your determination to "win." Winning isn't everything. If you can get what you want and the other side still declares victory, can you manage that? Can your ego handle that? You will negotiate with people obsessed with a "win." You will negotiate with egotists. You can use that. Contain your own ego and find ways for the egotist to declare victory, and you are more likely to get what you want.

Nerves in the negotiation context means you are paying attention to tension, ridding yourself of it and paying attention to the other side's tension points. Tensions run high in negotiations. There is finality to it all. There is a grade at the end. People will judge you and them based upon your perceived win or loss. Oftentimes the other side will play games. The other side may seek to increase your tension. Breathing and approaching negotiations empty and in the moment will keep your mind clear to succeed.

Tempo in the negotiation context means you will use pace as a tool in getting to resolution. This can start with the very beginning. Some will use arrival times to show their interest in reaching agreement. If you arrive early, you are sending a message that you want to reach agreement. If you arrive late, you may be sending the message that you don't care if a deal happens. During negotiations, how quickly you reply to an offer or counteroffer sends a message. Tempo in your communication sends a willingness or unwillingness to deal. Matching someone else's speech patterns can send a signal that you want to do something together. Speaking quickly or over someone is an aggressive move that would imply you have the upper hand. So the tempo of your actions and communications plays a role in getting deals done.

EXERCISE

1. Before negotiating your next deal, try to break it down into pieces. Instead of using a word type document, use an excel type document. Take any objective you are trying to reach in a negotiation and see if you can break it down into smaller chunks.

2. Before your next negotiation, use ARE U PRESENT to prepare. Write down or take electronic notes of each of the elements of the acronym. Are you perfectly aware of what you or your company wants? Write it down. Are you receptive and willing to compromise? What in particular are you focused on? Be sensitive to the need to engage and have a fair back and forth. Remember, great long-term relationship deals do not come from approaching with the objective of crushing the other side. On understanding, constantly work to confirm and clarify agreements and disagreements and work to see the deal from their perspective. Don't give up. Be persistent.

3. Continue through the acronym and use ARE U PRESENT as an outline for your negotiation strategy.

SUGGESTED DIALOGUE

"Before we get started, we would appreciate trying to understand your objectives in this negotiation. Can you share with us your 'mandate' from management?"

CHAPTER 18

LISTENING AND REMEMBERING

THERE IS A strong and dynamic relationship between listening and remembering. You simply cannot remember something you never heard in the first place. If you have a significant other and he or she tells you about a date for some commitment or obligation, and that date comes about and you claim you didn't know about it, what does the person say? He or she says, "I told you. You just don't remember." And you say, "You didn't tell me." And then the person tells you exactly when he or she told you. And now you are sort of remembering that conversation, but you never "heard" it in the first place. You were partially tuned in to it.

Chester Santos is a U.S. Memory Champion. Chester has memorized remarkable things like the entire membership of Congress, their party affiliation, their district, the committees on which they serve, and other volumes of information. Chester can memorize two hundred names of people he has just met. But Chester will tell you he can't remember a thing if he doesn't really listen and focus on it in the first place. That is one of the secrets of how these memory champions remember names; they listen intently and truly engage with the person by, among other things, repeating the name and associating it with something they already remember.

Knowing the various types of listening and listening tactics to remember names is another example of an invaluable soft skills tool. To remember someone's name, you listen to it carefully, you take in the person with a big focus, and you look for features that will help you remember the person. Perhaps the person resembles someone you already know with the same name. You repeat the name, smile, and shake the person's hand. You get a sense of him and tie his name to that sense. That is it. The person who puts forth that effort and hones those skills is exactly the kind of person who takes a room. That is exactly the type of person who moves ahead in organizations.

How important is learning and remembering someone's name? Perhaps the greatest and best-known teacher of soft skills was Dale Carnegie. He said, "Remember that a person's name is to that person the sweetest and most important sound in any language." It is one of Carnegie's top tips. It is a key to getting people receptive to you. It is a key to engaging with others.

When you study martial arts, whether it be Karate, Jiu Jitsu, Iaido, Systema, or any other art, you don't have the luxury of writing techniques down as you learn them. They are taught verbally as they have been passed on that way for centuries. It is part of the tradition. A teacher instructs you in a technique and you immediately perform the technique. You perform that technique over and over and over—until you have memorized it. The teacher performs it as many times as you need to recite it physically back to the teacher. At that time, at that moment as you listen, as you give and take, as you get confirmation, you are at a very high level of absorption and you will remember.

A legitimate black belt test from a demanding school with a strong lineage takes hours. And during those hours you are executing on techniques you have only heard in your head and practiced and rehearsed over a long period of time.

The stakes for listening and not listening in a martial arts dojo are high. You can get seriously hurt if you don't pay attention. You will get hit if you don't understand a block that you are to perform. You don't have the option of whether or not to get in a "zone." You get in the "zone" or you get knocked out.

For a martial artist, getting in "the zone" means being in the moment. If you are truly in the moment, you won't miss anything. In the moment, everything moves in slow motion. You take everything in. It is like a motion picture where you see the individual frames. That is how martial artists remember so much material. They are focused and in the moment. And that training serves them well in a sparring match or confrontation, because that same "in the moment" experience allows them to see things others don't see.

After several months of intense martial arts training students may notice something peculiar. For my own part, I noticed birds flying and my focus moving to their wings and bodies as they moved through the air. I could actually see their wings move. This was due to my intense focus on and interaction in martial arts training with things in motion.

I found the same true of people. I could see them move. I could sense how they would move next and maybe even what they would say next. I truly existed in a different zone. I was functioning at a different level and pace.

When memory experts like Chester are memorizing faces, random numbers, or decks of cards, they are in that moment. When you are in the moment, you are in touch with the Force or whatever you want to call it. When you are in the moment, you are something to behold and people will seem different to you. If you can engage with them in that moment, you will glow.

In response to this way of remembering, people often wonder, "Why don't you just take notes?" The problem with taking notes is that the act of taking notes during a human interaction can actually itself be a distraction, especially on a sales call. As you go through your business life, especially as you sit in meetings, presentations, and sales calls, you will often find yourself wishing you had a hidden recorder so you could truly listen, get the big picture, participate, and not have to take notes. You could just listen to the recording later. To take notes, you have to stop participating and look down to write, away from the speaker or speakers or audiences who are your coworkers, superiors, or customers.

Lacking the ability to record the meeting or conversation, most people will try to take notes as they sit in a sales call or in a meeting. In a modern meeting, you may take notes by hand on a piece of paper, by typing directly into a laptop or PDA, by scribbling on a modern electronic pad, or some combination of these. I have tried all these note-taking methods, and each time I found that while I was transcribing, I was often missing something else.

Meetings and sales calls are not like classes in school. At school, you are being presented with information with the understanding that you will take notes during the lecture. Good professors will even watch as a class takes notes, and time their cadence to the rhythm of those who are following along. Instructors will pause to make sure you have transcribed into your notes that all-important point they have made, so you can recite it on an exam. Good luck with this on a sales call. Just when you are about to write something down, several things will be mentioned that you will miss or the client will be looking for that all important body language of a nod.

Selling is about changing behavior. You can't change behavior if people don't respect you. And if you can get them to admire you, they will—or are much more likely to—buy from you. Selling is still an emotional experience between buyer and seller, no matter how technical the underlying product or service. One of the best ways to have someone admire you is to have superior listening and remembering skills and use them during the sales call. This is not just because it is cool; it also allows you to use professional selling techniques, because if you remember all of their pain points or challenges and opportunities, you can introduce the benefits of your service or product seamlessly into the conversation.

We can't carry a recorder into a sales meeting or other important business event. Listening and remembering is a hallmark of greatness. Work on your listening skills and translate customer needs into jargon you remember as a form of active listening. Know the names, personalities and roles of those with whom you will engage. Get your right brain into the game to blow away your buyers with your keen focus and photographic memory. If you feel the need to have a pencil and paper in front of you to show respect, you can do that, but your listening will be better if you don't look down to make a note. I have tried this no-notes technique in several key sales to very large companies. In each case, the prospects asked me how I remembered everything they said when I summarized at the end. I simply said, "I listened. We listen."

EXERCISE

1. **Practice active listening that translates needs into your industry jargon.** When you hear something important, you need to repeat it, not in the same words, but capturing the same meaning. And when you do this, use words that you will remember. Example: Suppose you are selling staffing services. The prospect says, "We need our jobs filled within three days." You say, "Okay, I got it, your SLA for time to fill is 72 hours." "SLA," "time to fill," and the hours are all language from staffing that you are more likely to remember. You have not only understood their requirements, you have also shown you know what you are doing. Now all you really have to remember is 72 hours. The rest will come to you.

2. **Know the people you are meeting, who they are and what they do.** Use LinkedIn and other

social media and search sites. You don't have to be one of those creepy anonymous stalkers. It is perfectly okay for someone to know you checked his or her profile. It is good that you want to know about your prospect. You will be respected for doing your homework. If someone comes to meet me and doesn't check me out on LinkedIn, I tend to respect the person less. If a person says he checked on LinkedIn and did it anonymously, what is he trying to hide? The better you know the players, the more likely you will remember what they say because you can associate what they say with who they are.

3. **Memorize the roles of those you're meeting before the meeting.** If you go into a sales call and don't know the names, background, and organizational roles of those you are trying to sell, shame on you. You'd better take notes because my techniques won't help you. You are entitled to know who will be in the meeting and what role they play, and you need to do your research on them. Knowing their role is absolutely critical because you have to communicate very differently based on their role. Example: Suppose you are selling billing services. And suppose there is a procurement representative, a CFO, a CIO, and an accounts receivable clerk. The procurement person cares

about price; the CFO cares about functionality risk, price, compatibility, and scalability; the CIO cares about system integrity and software compatibility; and the A/R clerk who will be using the tool cares about functionality. Work to sell the A/R clerk on price? The clerks mostly don't care about price, they are looking for the new tool that will make their life easier. Try to sell the procurement person on the great features and it'll fall on deaf ears. If you know the roles, you will remember who says what because the things they say are predictable based on their roles in the organization. Someone who has responsibility for budgets is very different than someone who wants to buy something to make their work easier.

4. **Study the room and players as you walk in and notice any unique features.** You can then associate these unique features with a point you want to remember. Suppose there is a conference phone and it has a unique shape. You can actually visualize the phone and store points on each side of the phone for remembering later. Suppose the leader of the meeting is wearing purple. Use it to remember something. What memory experts do well is use the right side of their brain. The left side of the brain is where we mostly live and what

we mostly use. Language, math, and analytical thinking all take place in the left half of our brain. The right side is where creativity and images reside. Memory experts use images to help them remember long lists that cannot be easily memorized with analytical thinking. Using the color purple to remember something integrates your right brain into the meeting. I recommend that you study memorization. It is an invaluable skill. Right-brain techniques are powerful tools that with a little training and practice can set you apart.

5. **Create a story out of the needs of the customer.** Stories are easier to remember than lists. Use your right brain to create a story about the need, challenge, or opportunity of the prospect. Example: Suppose you are selling radio advertising and having trouble because the prospect tried radio advertising once, spent a bunch of money, and got no new sales. You might imagine a van bearing the company's name and a radio antenna on top of the van spewing dollar bills into the street. They go straight into the gutter. Again, this is a right-brain technique that will help you remember the problem and challenge associated with your prospect.

SUGGESTED DIALOGUE

Remembering peoples' names is a great way to help you remember what is said. It gives you something to hang stuff on. Here is suggested dialogue to help with that. Always ask someone, "What is your name?" Suppose she says, "I am Jane." You say, "Hi Jane, I am Bob." Then, after repeating the person's name, say "Nice to meet you Jane." You either want to link her to a Jane you know or find some physical accessory or feature you can use to cement the name in your mind. "I have a cousin named Jane." Or, "I really like your watch, Jane, how did you find that?"

CHAPTER 19

YOUR TWELVE-WEEK LISTENING IMPROVEMENT PLAN ("LIP")

YOUR LIP INVOLVES twelve of my favorite exercises which you practice each day of a twelve-week period. If you follow this practice and these exercises, you will transform yourself. You will be treated differently. You will notice people suggesting you for leadership positions. You will be promoted more quickly. You will receive raises more quickly. You will improve and advance every area of your life. You will become a leader by having become a Samurai Listener.

Week 1:   ARE U PRESENT

Week 2:   Awareness—Practice the Big Picture

Week 3:   Receptive—Identify and Reduce Bias

Week 4:   Engaged—Study and Practice Give and
Take and Avoid Interruptions

Week 5:   Understanding—Practice Active
Listening

Week 6:   Persistence—Staying the Course

Week 7:   Resolution—Confirming Takeaways

Week 8:   Emotions—Getting in Touch with and
Managing Emotions

Week 9:   Senses—Broadening your Awareness
with Other Senses

Week 10: Ego—Managing Your Own and Others

Week 11: Nerves and Tension—Spotting It in
Others and Managing It in Yourself

Week 12: Tempo—Mastering the Dance

Week 1: ARE U PRESENT

Each day, preferably in the morning, watch and listen to a great leader, someone you admire, who is interacting with others. YouTube is probably the best tool to use because you can watch it when it is convenient and find plenty of material on your favorite speaker. Find clips where the leaders answer questions because answering a question involves having to listen. Watch how they clarify questions before they respond. Press conferences are ideal and provide you with an opportunity to do this. Do this every day for the first seven days of your first week. Take notes observing the techniques they use and integrate them into your practices. I like to watch Tony Blair interviews because I met him once and thought he was a great communicator. Others might like to watch Ronald Reagan. If you are a businessperson you may like Jack Welch. But whoever you admire, spend time watching them personally interact with others.

Memorize the acronym ARE U PRESENT and put the phrase next to your computer screen or on your computer screen. Make it a screensaver.

Week 2: Awareness–Practice Getting the Big Picture

Set an alarm on your PDA device to tell you to step back from your screen and get the big picture. Take a walk and widen your perspective. The walk is good for you too. When you are part of a group discussion, don't just focus on the person speaking. Expand your view to watch how others are listening and responding. Use this exercise to expand your field of vision so you can take in how others are reacting to her or him. Move from person to person while keeping the speaker in your gaze as well. When you see "talking heads" on a news channel, don't just look at the person speaking. Train yourself to observe others' reactions to the speaker, including the hosts. Think like the cameraperson who directs the cameras and take lots of shots from multiple perspectives, to get to the heart of what is going on, not just the face of the speaker.

Week 3: Receptive–Identify and Reduce Bias

You need to understand your potential biases. Each day, think about someone you like and someone you don't like. Write down their names (remember to throw this away when you are done!). What don't you like about the people who annoy you? What caused you to stop liking them? What annoys you about them? Now consider someone you like. What do you like about them? As rational as you may feel in not liking or liking some person, I am going to tell you that these people are important to you because what you don't like and like can indicate a bias, and that bias is something that is holding you back. The very trait that you associate with the person you don't like? This trait will cause you not to like others with that trait and, as we implicitly learned at Leadership School when I was young, this will cause you not to like people with that trait or even with the same name. This reflection will help you greatly reduce your bias towards others. Spend your week on this analysis and understanding.

Document the conversational style of those you listen to frequently. Understanding that people have different communication styles and recording what you learn from each engagement is invaluable to making you a Samurai Listener. Keep a journal of your insights and study it before you engage with them the next time.

Week 4: Engaged–Study and Practice Give and Take and Avoid Interruptions

Pick someone you know to be a slow talker and engage with this person. Pick someone you know who rambles and engage with him. Pick someone you know who dominates conversations and engage with her. Pick someone you know who is an introvert and engage with the person. Don't try to nudge the slow talker along; let him move at his own pace. The person could be an introvert. Breathe and give him the time to develop and express his thoughts. Remember the story of the tortoise and the hare. And when you engage someone, slow down yourself. Matching speech patterns is a very effective sales and communication strategy. Make sure your exchanges are fair. During this week try to keep track of how many sentences you speak compared to the other person. Instead of competing for airtime or dominating conversations yourself, work for fair exchanges. People will appreciate time with you.

Week 5: Understanding–Practice Perspective Listening; Practice Active Listening

Go to the movies with a friend, someone who will practice with you, someone who also wants to be a better listener or communicator. It would be ideal if you pick a friend with a different perspective, maybe very different, from you. If you are a woman, go with a man. If you are young, find someone older. If you are white, go with someone from a different race or ethnicity. If you are straight, pick a friend that is LGBTQ. Go see a movie together and then discuss it in a structured way. Try to pick a movie that emphasizes differences. Maybe use the following questions or something like them: What was the point of the movie? Who was the character you identified with the most? The least? What other movie that you have seen was it most similar to? Would you recommend it to others? If so, how would you describe it?

In your conversations or exchanges this week, try to limit yourself to questions only. If this seems too awkward or difficult for you, then make your statements very limited in number so that the vast majority of what you say in the conversation or meeting is questions. Becoming good at asking questions doesn't make you annoying, it makes you a wonderful companion—it shows you care. Great leaders ask lots of questions.

Week 6: Persistence–Staying the Course

The biggest impediment to sticking with a conversation or speaker or meeting is what is in our heads. Make a daily list of what is on your mind. Certainly before a major conversation, meeting, sales call, or interview, breathe and be aware of your tension. What is bothering you? What is on your mind? Write it down on paper if you use that or on your notes app if you use one. This will allow you to clear your mind. If you come into a conversation with tension or other things on your mind, even unrelated to the speaker, you will not get much out of listening to the speaker. These tensions are often the result of something else we are thinking about so it is important to get those things somewhere where we can think about them later. Tidy up your head to stay focused.

Week 7: Resolution–Confirming Takeaways

During this week, prepare your pre- and post-listening rituals. What will you do before and after the exchange? Design a system of showing respect before and after an exchange. Think about the Japanese bow and what a great respect that is. As you finish the exchange, express your thankfulness and respect. Finish the exchange by reviewing key points or takeaways. Imagine yourself in the martial arts circle. What did you appreciate about the exchange? What did you learn? What could you now teach someone else?

Week 8: Emotions–Getting in Touch with and Managing Emotions

During this week, identify someone in your circle that you think of as tending to be "defensive" or someone who blames others. Learn to step up and be assertive and take the blame, even if it is only partially your fault. It is easy and will soften your exchanges. In your conversations this week, practice saying, "I'm sorry." Practice saying, "It was my fault."

Week 9: Senses–Broadening Your Awareness with Other Senses

Walking and breathing are the best ways to master your breath work. Take a step, breathe in; then take another step, and breathe out. Continue this practice of one step/one breath in and one step/one breath out. You can extend these to two steps breathing in, and two steps breathing out, and mix them up. Try to inhale on one step and exhale on two. Find patterns that make you feel better. At different times, different strategies will feel different to you. You can build up your energy with fewer steps and calm yourself with long breaths associated with multiple steps.

Week 10: Ego–Managing Your Own and Others

For this week, put yourself in an environment where you are forced to interact with strangers. Join a new club. Volunteer for a nonprofit or for an event. If you manage others, find a servant role. Help rebuild homes after a disaster. Get out of your bubble where everybody kisses your behind. Spend some time with your worst critics. Attend a summer camp without your friends around. Go back to school.

Week 11: Nerves and Tension–Spotting It in Others and Managing It in Yourself

This week, every morning when you wake up and every night as you go to bed, practice segmented tension exercises. Begin at your feet and as you breathe in flex your feet as hard as you can while leaving the rest of your body soft. Isolate each of your limbs as you progress up your body. Flex your legs, flex your buttocks, flex your abs, flex your chest, flex your arms, flex your back, flex your shoulders, and flex your neck, each time relaxing all else. This isolation technique will help you learn what relaxation and tension feel like. Over time, you probably accept feeling tense as normal. This exercise should cleanse you of those sensations so you can recognize tension when it happens.

Week 12: Tempo–Mastering the Dance

Great conversation is like a beautiful dance or a wonderfully executed martial arts kata. Select the music style that you think best resembles your speech patterns. If you speak quickly, it may be rock or hip-hop. If you speak slowly, it may be smooth jazz or country. Now, during this week study all the people with whom you interact. What is their rhythm? What music could they speak to if music were playing? As you make note of these paces, record them in your memory or in your notes app or journal. When you see them, that music should play as a reminder of their rhythm.

CHAPTER 20

CONCLUSION—
DO YOU FEEL ME
NOW?

OUR EDUCATIONAL SYSTEM separates physical activity from learning. Except for lunch, recess, or gym, you're at your desk and supposed to use your minds. This forced dichotomy continues for most people as they advance in their careers, regardless of their professions.

However, as I've stressed throughout this book, I feel strongly that the link between physical martial arts training and practice and interactions within the workplace reunites the mind and the body in a way that can improve your interactions with others. Broadening your sense of awareness, improving your receptiveness, engaging others in a conscious, fair, and positive way, showing understanding through dialog, persistently staying with those with whom you are engaged, agreeing upon takeaways, understanding the role of emotions, using all of your senses, keeping egos in check, managing nerves and tension, and getting into the groove of the dance will make you someone people want to interact with and follow.

The key to success with these principles doesn't come from just learning of them. Changing human behavior is a real challenge, even if you are just trying to change yourself. If you follow the twelve-week plan, you will enhance your soft skills. You will become a Samurai Listener.

ABOUT THE AUTHOR

STEVEN "CASH" NICK-
ERSON is president and
a principal of PDS Tech,
Inc., a position he has
held for fourteen years.
With approximately
$400 million in annual
sales, PDS is one of the
largest engineering and
IT staffing firms in the
United States, employing
over 10,000 employees
annually. Nickerson has
held a variety of legal

and executive positions in his 30-year career, includ-
ing serving as an attorney and marketing executive for
Union Pacific Railroad, an associate and then partner at
Jenner & Block (one of Chicago's five largest law firms),
and chairman and CEO of an internet company he took
public through a reverse merger.

An avid writer and speaker on the workplace, the jobs, economy, and employment, Nickerson is the author of *BOOMERangs, Engaging the Aging Workforce in America* (2014), *StagNation, Understanding the New Normal in Employment* (2013), *Getting To Next, Lessons to Help Take Your Career to The Next Level* (2015), and *Listening as a Martial Art* (2015). He also writes travel books including *A Texan in Tuscany* (2013).

Cash Nickerson holds a JD and MBA from Washington University in St. Louis where he was an editor of the law review and a recipient of the US Steel Scholarship. He is a member of the National Council of Washington University in St. Louis School of Law and International Council of the Whitney R. Harris World Law Institute. Nickerson serves on the Equifax Workforce Solutions Client Advisory Board and was Keynote speaker at the Equifax 2013 Client Forum. Nickerson was honored with the Distinguished Alumni Award in 2013 by Washington University in St. Louis School of Law and a Founders Day Distinguished Alumni Award from Washington University in St. Louis in 2014. He received the Global Philanthropy Award in 2010 from Washington University in St. Louis for his support of the Crimes Against Humanity Initiative. Nickerson was elected the Ethan A. H. Shepley Trustee at Washington University in St. Louis in December 2014 for a four year term.

Cash Nickerson is licensed to practice law in California, Nevada, Illinois, Nebraska, and Texas and is a member of the American, Los Angeles, Austin, and Dallas Bar Associations. He is an avid martial artist, ranked as a third-degree Black Belt in Kenpo Karate, a Brown Belt in Brazilian Jiu Jitsu, and a Russian Martial Art instructor at his school, Big D Systema in Dallas.

Mr. Nickerson has appeared on numerous talk radio shows including NPR, *The Joe Elliot Show*, Americas Evening News, Lifestyle Talk Radio, *The Lifestyle Show*, *Conversations with Peter Solomon*, Ringside Politics, *The Dave Malarkey Show*, *The Morning Show*, and *The Costa Report*.